QUICK WIN PUBLIC RELATIONS

Answers to your top 100 public relations questions

Kevin Hora

·OAK·TREE·PRESS·

Published by
OAK TREE PRESS
19 Rutland Street, Cork, Ireland
www.oaktreepress.com

© 2014 Kevin Hora

A catalogue record of this book is
available from the British Library.

ISBN 978 1 78119 122 4 (Paperback)
ISBN 978 1 78119 123 1 (PDF)
ISBN 978 1 78119 124 8 (ePub)
ISBN 978 1 78119 125 5 (Kindle)

INTRODUCTION

Quick Win Public Relations is aimed at businesses and not-for-profit organisations seeking to build and enhance their relationships with key stakeholders across a range of activities, from publicity to managing crises. It is especially helpful for small and medium-sized enterprises and owner-managed businesses. Further and higher education students, and students on professional courses, will find it an invaluable study aid, while educators will find it a useful quick reference guide.

The book is divided into five sections, designed to take you from basic understanding of essential concepts, through practical ability in handling PR tactics, to creative and strategic practices that can make organisations and practitioners stand apart as excellent communicators:

- **PR Essentials** helps you to understand what public relations is really about, offering easy-to-grasp introductions to relationship and reputation management, engaging with publics, and different uses of PR. It also shows how PR complements the marketing and human resources functions within your organisation, and the role it plays in enabling you to communicate more effectively with external publics;

- **Engaging with Professionals** contains useful tips and techniques for building good relationships with journalists, photographers and graphic designers. With easy-to-follow advice on organising media events, you will be able to enhance the quality of your media work and gain better coverage;

- **Practical PR Skills** focuses on the essential writing skills that form every practitioner's basic armoury – press releases, holding statements, feature articles, photograph captions and speeches;

- **Engaging Online** has become vital to the success of any organisation's communications, and this section provides a practical guide to different types of social media, including the use of podcasts and blogs;

- **PR Excellence** takes you on a whistlestop tour of advanced strategies. Beginning with internal communication audits, the section delves into reputation management, implementing corporate social responsibility (CSR) programmes, lobbying, activism, and issues and crisis management.

Each section contains useful 'Hints' boxes and mini case studies 'In Practice', which use examples of excellent PR practice to illustrate key points. The sections can be read in sequence, growing progressively more complex and strategic, or may be dipped in and out of as needs arise. As an alternative, you can focus on specific topics using the grid in the Contents pages. Each question is cross-referenced with others to build a more complete understanding of the topic.

Good public relations practice is not something to be achieved overnight: successful PR is much more a marathon than a sprint. Enjoy applying the techniques and tips you read here to your own organisation; and enjoy the journey towards creating excellent relationships with your key publics. Above all, let me wish you many quick wins and continued success in your PR efforts.

Kevin Hora
Dublin, January 2014

CONTENTS

Search by theme:

PR Essentials	**1**
Engaging with Professionals	**55**
Practical PR Skills	**95**
Engaging Online	**119**
PR Excellence	**145**

Or search by topic:

Definitions
External Publics
Internal Publics
Management
Operational
Planning
Specialisms
using the grid overleaf.

About the Author	**191**
The Quick Win series	**192**

PR ESSENTIALS	Definitions	External Publics	Internal Publics	Management	Operational	Planning	Specialisms	PAGE
Q1 What is public relations?	☑							2
Q2 What can PR do for my organisation?		☑	☑		☑			4
Q3 What are the most commonly used public relations activities?		☑	☑		☑			6
Q4 How do I know who my publics are?		☑	☑					8
Q5 How do I prioritise my publics?		☑	☑					9
Q6 What is relationship management?	☑	☑	☑					11
Q7 What is reputation management?	☑	☑	☑					13
Q8 How do I manage reputation?		☑	☑	☑				15
Q9 How do PR and human resource management complement each other?			☑			☑		17
Q10 Why should I use PR to communicate with staff?			☑					19
Q11 What are the main tools of internal communications?			☑		☑			21
Q12 What is the difference between PR and marketing?		☑			☑	☑		23
Q13 What is integrated marketing communication?		☑			☑	☑		24
Q14 What does PR do for brands that advertising and marketing do not?		☑			☑	☑		26

PR ESSENTIALS	Definitions	External Publics	Internal Publics	Management	Operational	Planning	Specialisms	PAGE
Q15 How do I manage sponsorship effectively?		☑		☑	☑	☑		28
Q16 What will celebrity endorsements do for my organisation?		☑			☑	☑		30
Q17 What events are good for promotion and publicity?		☑			☑	☑		32
Q18 What is a pseudo-event?	☑	☑			☑	☑		34
Q19 Are publicity stunts useful?		☑			☑	☑		35
Q20 What is controlled media?	☑	☑			☑	☑		37
Q21 What is financial PR?	☑	☑					☑	39
Q22 What is litigation PR?	☑	☑					☑	41
Q23 What is community PR?	☑	☑					☑	43
Q24 I need to write a PR plan – is there a model I can follow?					☑			45
Q25 Where can I find PR campaign case studies, just to give me some ideas?					☑			47
Q26 How do I carry out a situation analysis?					☑	☑		48
Q27 What is boundary spanning in PR?	☑				☑			50
Q28 How do I evaluate my PR efforts?				☑				51
Q29 I'm not very creative – will my PR efforts suffer?					☑	☑		53

ENGAGING WITH PROFESSIONALS	Definitions	External Publics	Internal Publics	Management	Operational	Planning	Specialisms	PAGE
Q30 How do I build a relationship with journalists?		☑			☑			56
Q31 How do I decide what media to contact with a press release?		☑			☑			58
Q32 Are alternative media a bit *too* alternative for my needs?		☑			☑			60
Q33 How do I pitch a story to the media?		☑			☑			61
Q34 How does a journalist decide what is news?		☑			☑			63
Q35 What timeframe should I consider for sending material to the media?		☑			☑			65
Q36 What is an embargo?	☑	☑			☑			67
Q37 Why won't a journalist accept my press kit and free samples?		☑			☑			68
Q38 What does on the record, off the record, and non-attributable mean?	☑	☑			☑			70
Q39 How does citizen journalism affect my organisation?	☑	☑			☑	☑		71
Q40 What is a media briefing?	☑	☑			☑			73

ENGAGING WITH PROFESSIONALS

	Definitions	External Publics	Internal Publics	Management	Operational	Planning	Specialisms	PAGE
Q41 When could I use narrowcasting instead of broadcasting?		☑			☑	☑		74
Q42 What is media monitoring?	☑	☑			☑			76
Q43 How do I organise a press conference?		☑			☑			78
Q44 How do I organise a photo call?		☑			☑			79
Q45 How do I organise a facility visit?		☑			☑			80
Q46 How do I brief a photographer?		☑			☑			82
Q47 How do I brief a graphic designer for a print publication?		☑			☑			84
Q48 How do I brief a web designer for a company website?		☑			☑			86
Q49 What is the role of the PR practitioner?	☑					☑		88
Q50 What are the attributes and skills of a PR practitioner?	☑					☑		90
Q51 Should I hire a PR consultancy or do the job myself?					☑	☑		92
Q52 Should I consider hiring freelancers to help my PR efforts?					☑	☑		94

PRACTICAL PR SKILLS	Definitions	External Publics	Internal Publics	Management	Operational	Planning	Specialisms	PAGE
Q53 What do I put into a press kit?		☑			☑			96
Q54 What's the secret of a good press release?		☑			☑			97
Q55 What should I avoid when writing a press release?		☑			☑			99
Q56 What content goes in a holding statement?		☑			☑			101
Q57 Can I write a feature article and use it for publicity purposes?		☑			☑			102
Q58 What makes a good publicity photograph?		☑			☑			104
Q59 When should I write an extended picture caption for a photograph?		☑			☑			106
Q60 What content should go in a newsletter or e-zine?		☑			☑			108
Q61 What is an advertorial?	☑	☑			☑			110
Q62 How do I write a speech?		☑	☑		☑			111
Q63 How do I write a speech for somebody else to deliver?		☑	☑		☑			113
Q64 How do I prepare for a broadcast interview?		☑			☑			115

ENGAGING ONLINE	Definitions	External Publics	Internal Publics	Management	Operational	Planning	Specialisms	PAGE
Q65 What social media sites can I use for PR?		☑			☑			120
Q66 How do I use social media for building relationships?		☑			☑			123
Q67 How do I publicise my presence on social media?		☑			☑			125
Q68 How do I use social media for promotions?		☑			☑			127
Q69 What is a blog?	☑	☑			☑			129
Q70 Is writing a blog hard?		☑			☑			131
Q71 Why will people want to listen to my podcast?		☑			☑			133
Q72 What is a dark site?	☑	☑			☑			135
Q73 What is an electronic press kit?	☑	☑			☑			137
Q74 Should I control which employees can update my social media accounts?		☑			☑			139
Q75 How does search engine optimisation work?		☑			☑			141
Q76 Why can porosity be bad for an organisation?		☑			☑			143

PR EXCELLENCE	Definitions	External Publics	Internal Publics	Management	Operational	Planning	Specialisms	PAGE
Q77 What is a communications audit?	☑			☑	☑	☑		146
Q78 How do I carry out a communications audit?					☑	☑		148
Q79 How do I establish my organisation's corporate identity?				☑	☑	☑		150
Q80 How do I protect my organisation's corporate identity?					☑	☑		152
Q81 What is corporate social responsibility?	☑	☑			☑	☑		154
Q82 What kind of activities can be used in corporate social responsibility?		☑			☑	☑		156
Q83 What is greenwashing?	☑				☑	☑		158
Q84 What is astroturfing?	☑				☑	☑		159
Q85 What is lobbying?	☑						☑	160
Q86 How do I lobby a public authority?	☑				☑	☑		162
Q87 What is activism?	☑				☑	☑		164
Q88 What tactics can I use in an activist campaign?					☑	☑		166
Q89 How do I respond to an activist campaign?					☑	☑		168
Q90 What is an issue?					☑	☑		170
Q91 What is issues management?					☑	☑		171

PR EXCELLENCE	Definitions	External Publics	Internal Publics	Management	Operational	Planning	Specialisms	PAGE
Q92 What is a crisis?					☑	☑		173
Q93 What is crisis management?					☑	☑		175
Q94 How do I prepare to manage a crisis?					☑	☑		177
Q95 What goes in my crisis kit?					☑	☑		179
Q96 How should I respond to a crisis?					☑	☑		181
Q97 Should the most senior manager always be the spokesperson during a crisis?					☑	☑		183
Q98 What is the difference between an apologia and an apology as a response to a crisis?	☑				☑	☑		185
Q99 How do I use PR to lessen the damage caused by a product recall?					☑	☑		187
Q100 How do I rebuild my organisation's reputation after a crisis?					☑	☑		189

PR ESSENTIALS

Q1   What is public relations?

Public relations (PR) is a widely used and misunderstood term. You may be familiar with different roles in PR, including:

- The PRO of an amateur sports club who sends match reports to local journalists;
- The marketing manager who uses sponsorship to create product awareness and generate sales;
- The publicist who keeps celebrity clients highly exposed in the media.

But these are only a very small part of PR practice, and do not give an understanding of the big picture.

Public relations is:

- **A management function:** It is concerned with managing relationships with publics;
- **A strategic function:** It is concerned with where your organisation is, and where it wants to be;
- **An intelligence-gathering and advisory function:** It examines your organisation's internal and external environments, anticipates trends and issues, and advises management on how to deal with them;
- **A planned activity or activity:** Lucky breaks like winning an award create publicity, but are quickly forgotten; planning creates long-term results;
- **Based on communication and negotiation:** It creates a dialogue with publics that builds goodwill and mutual understanding;
- Concerned with a broad range of business, social, political and environmental issues.

It is not:

- **Marketing and promotions:** They share common features, but PR has many more functions;

- **Spin:** Usually used in political communication, the word now includes any attempt to put a deceptively positive slant on a bad story;

- **Propaganda:** Although it derives from the Latin for 'to propagate' and once had a similar meaning to PR, it is now used inaccurately as a derogatory word to describe PR. Propaganda has no concern for the truth – PR should;

- **A career you enter because you are 'good with people':** Apart from being a hermit, is there any job that does not require this?

See also

Q2   What can PR do for my organisation?
Q3   What are the most commonly used PR activities?

Q2   What can PR do for my organisation?

Some organisations use PR in a slipshod way:

- Occasional promotion to support the marketing department;
- Fire-fighting during a crisis;
- Sending out press releases with little news value;
- Hiring a celebrity for a product launch.

This PR is done for short-term objectives, and only produces short-term benefits at best.

Compared to advertising and marketing, PR is very cost-effective communication – sometimes virtually free, so any organisation can afford it. PR messages have more credibility than marketing and advertising messages, and often have longer lasting effects as well.

PR can increase awareness of your organisation, its activities, products and staff, help build sales, market share and brands, prevent problems, and more.

The long-term benefits of PR – relationships, reputation, goodwill – are only achieved when your organisation commits wholeheartedly to it. Every policy, strategy and activity you undertake must consider how your publics will react. That takes much effort and time. But, eventually, awareness of PR becomes part of your organisation's culture.

When every employee considers how their actions affect your publics, PR will have become an integral way of thinking in your organisation. Credibility and goodwill are gained, and your organisation can shape public opinion through open dialogue with its publics.

Your organisation should be:

- Truthful and trustworthy;
- Committed to communicating with publics;
- Alert to the possibilities and challenges that benefit or threaten relationships.

Rather than *doing* public relations, your organisation *achieves* public relations.

From the small corner shop to the multinational corporation, PR helps organisations to achieve one key goal: building and maintaining relationships.

See also
Q1 What is public relations?
Q3 What are the most commonly used PR activities?

Q3   What are the most commonly used public relations activities?

Activities depend on the type of organisation, and what it wants to achieve. Technology start-up companies use different activities to long-established charities; political parties to music festivals. If everybody used the same few activities, PR would be of little use.

Some of the more common activities can be categorised under key headings:

Area of activity	Examples
Media	Media relations. Press releases, photographs, feature articles. Press kits. Press conferences, one-to-one interviews, briefings. Media monitoring.
Events	Trade and consumer shows. Open houses, samplings, demonstrations. Conferences, seminars. Hospitality.
Direct communication	Shareholder AGMs and other meetings. Staff meetings. Email. Speaking engagements. Newsletters.
Online	Social media. Blogging. Podcasting. Interactive websites.
Promotions	Sponsorship. Stunts. Brochures, leaflets, corporate publications.

Area of activity	Examples
Specialised	Lobbying. Issues and crisis management. Corporate social responsibility (CSR) and community relations. Financial public relations.

This is not an exhaustive list, and there are hundreds of other activities to choose from. The challenge is to use the common activities well, and to constantly seek new activities to make your organisation stand out. Whatever you do, those activities should:

- Be appropriate to your skills and resources;
- Be familiar to you;
- Deliver measurable results;
- Be adaptable for use with different publics, or in different contexts;
- Be innovative, creative and effective.

See also
Q1   What is public relations?
Q17   What events are good for promotion and publicity?

Q4   How do I know who my publics are?

PR practitioners do not deal with the general public; they deal with specific internal and external publics. Deciding who these publics are is not difficult – it just takes time to think about the relationship your organisation has with different groups. Start by dividing them into categories, and list every public with whom your organisation has or would like a relationship. Many types of public will be common to most organisations.

Internal publics include employees, managers, directors, contractors, volunteers, trade unions and other representative groups, owners, shareholders and investors.

External publics are more wide-ranging:

- **Government:** Local, regional, national and international (the EU) parliaments, civil and public servants and regulators;
- **Commercial:** Customers, suppliers, business associates, distributors, rivals, chamber of commerce, industry associates and representatives;
- **Financial:** Banks and other financial institutions, shareholders, stock exchanges and brokers, and the financial media;
- **Community:** Residents' associations, local opinion formers, pressure and activist groups, local organisations (sports, cultural, educational, business) and local media.

Sometimes the word 'stakeholder' is used instead of publics. There is a fine distinction between the two words, however. Not all publics are stakeholders, but all stakeholders are publics. Stakeholders are publics who have a material interest in their relationship with the organisation, and on whom the organisation itself depends. They include shareholders, customers, staff, suppliers, distributors and business associates.

See also
Q5   How do I prioritise my publics?
Q6   What is relationship management?

Q5   How do I prioritise my publics?

Different publics take priority at different times for different reasons. This makes it difficult to know when to communicate routinely and when they need special attention. One way to know is by monitoring issues. There is a saying that issues create publics, so the PR boundary spanning role is useful.

Many practitioners divide publics into four categories, based on publics' awareness of an issue and how mobilised they are to address it. It is useful to see these categories as a way of building relationships too.

Category of public	Activity level	Priority for communication
Non-publics	These are uninterested and disinterested – they are publics that are unaware of the organisation's existence.	They have a low priority for communication, and only need to be monitored for changes in their level of awareness.
Latent publics	An issue or relationship with the organisation exists, but they are unaware of it.	These are low priority publics who can be communicated with gradually to build trust and address issues of concern and benefit.
Aware publics	These publics recognise that a relationship or an issue exists, but have made no organised effort to create a firm relationship.	These are medium priority publics. Regular communication creates a dialogue, maintains trust and addresses issues.

Category of public	Activity level	Priority for communication
Active publics	These publics are aware of a relationship or issue and actively engage with the organisation and comprise: • **Single-issue publics** are active on one issue or a single relationship that affects a small number of people; • **Hot-issue publics** are active on a single issue that is important to them; • **All-issue publics** are few in number, but their relationship with your organisation goes across a range of issues. For example, the local community as a public includes customers, employees, suppliers and rivals.	These are high priority publics, with whom you should be in constant communication.

See also

Q4   How do I know who my publics are?
Q6   What is relationship management?

Q6 What is relationship management?

Some practitioners believe that relationship management, not communication, is the main purpose of PR. Communication in all forms, then, is simply a tool that enables the PR manager to create and maintain relationships with publics that have the potential to enhance or constrain an organisation as it attempts to meet its goals.

On its own, communication may not be able to sustain a relationship: your organisation needs to behave in a way that demonstrates its commitment to its publics. For example, a pharmaceutical factory that trumpets its environmentally-friendly practices in glossy corporate brochures will find that this counts for little with publics if a chemical leak poisons the town water supply.

Every relationship between an organisation and a public has three main features:

- **Interdependence:** Both depend on each other to make the relationship work;
- **Exchange of information:** The relationship is built on a flow of information that creates transparency and trust;
- **Historical factors and future consequences:** Relationships are dynamic and constantly evolve. Knowing the results of past actions, and realising that every future action will have an effect in the relationship, helps you to remain aware of the delicate nature of a relationship.

Relationship management requires continuously engaging with publics, and meeting their expectations, not just telling them what management thinks they might like to hear.

See also
Q4 How do I know who my publics are?
Q5 How do I prioritise my publics?
Q21 What is financial public relations?
Q22 What is litigation public relations?

Q23   What is community PR?
Q79   How do I establish my organisation's corporate identity?
Q80   How do I protect my organisation's corporate identity?

Q7   What is reputation management?

Your organisation has a reputation to defend, live up to, or, indeed, improve. Reputation is formed from perceptions of whether your organisation is trustworthy, ethical, reliable and so on.

Because each public – and the individuals who comprise it – can have very different perceptions, your organisation has no control over its reputation, and cannot directly manage how it is perceived. Instead, it can only seek to influence public opinion.

Unlike relationship management, which involves publics who have a connection to your organisation, reputation management is concerned with publics who are merely aware of your organisation's existence. This means that reputation matters most with strangers – when relationships are formed with stakeholders, their impression of your organisation is strengthened.

Nonetheless, reputation management is important for organisations because:

- It creates a bank of goodwill among publics that can help during difficult periods or crises;
- Influential business and social opinion leaders, government agencies and regulators place higher trust in organisations with good reputations;
- It can help attract employees, volunteers and business associates;
- It enhances the credibility of key personnel, such as the CEO or directors;
- It can increase an organisation's financial or social value;
- It can differentiate brands and products from rivals;
- Scrutiny from consumers, regulators and the media highlights organisations whose bad reputations leave them vulnerable to loss of business or even closure.

See also

Q8   How do I manage reputation?

Q22   What is litigation PR?

Q79   How do I establish my organisation's corporate identity?

Q80   How do I protect my organisation's corporate identity?

Q100 How do I rebuild my organisation's reputation after a crisis?

Q8 How do I manage reputation?

Because reputation is a very individual perception of your organisation, it is not really possible to control how your organisation is perceived by publics. However, it is possible to communicate the core values you wish to have known about your organisation, and thus enhance public perception. It goes without saying that the communication should be factual and open a dialogue with publics; otherwise it will be quickly regarded as corporate propaganda and ignored or ridiculed.

Because your reputation is constantly evolving, you need to plan to present your organisation to publics:

- Identify publics with whom your organisation has no relationship, but who could influence other publics;
- Assess how those publics see the organisation;
- Identify the elements of your organisation's identity that you want to make known and understood;
- Identify differences between your organisation's identity and publics' perceptions;
- Plan the activities, behaviour and channels that will communicate core values to publics;
- Identify 'champions' who will be the public face of your campaign – the CEO, or employees who are prominent in their business or local communities, for instance;
- Evaluate the programme to assess whether your reputation has been enhanced, or to identify areas that did not work.

While communication can build a reputation, it takes time and effort, and can cost a good deal of money. Just as effective is the experience your organisation offers its publics. The day-to-day activities of your organisation may be mundane but, over time, they can develop into good practices, such as acting in a responsible and ethical way, that earn a reputation, and reduce the need for costly campaigns to reinforce it.

See also

Q7   What is reputation management?
Q79   How do I establish my organisation's corporate identity?
Q80   How do I protect my organisation's corporate identity?
Q100   How do I rebuild my organisation's reputation after a crisis?

Q9   How do PR and human resource management complement each other?

PR and human resource management (HRM) fulfil similar internal roles. The phrases 'internal communications' and 'employee relations' are sometimes used to describe how they complement each other. Employees are a vital public, and how you communicate with them can determine how well your reputation is protected.

The HR department should have control over all aspects of employee relations where the privacy of the employee is concerned, and in accordance with employment law. It also should have sole responsibility for setting the communications policy, though the PR department should contribute to the planning of this policy.

The PR department should have responsibility for implementing the policy, using its communications skills in managing intranets and websites, designing and publishing newsletters, and other internal communications activities.

In this approach, the HR department effectively becomes the client of the PR department, which is 'retained' for its strategic advice and tactical know-how.

Problems arise when the two departments fail to work together as the **In Practice** box shows.

In Practice

Retailer HMV learned the importance of employee relations after entering administration in 2013. When 190 employees were made redundant, the company's social media planner tweeted on the company's Twitter account: 'Mass execution of loyal employees'. This provoked a management response, which worsened matters. A later tweet read: 'Just overheard our Marketing Manager (he's staying, folks) ask: "How do I shut down Twitter?"'. HMV was ridiculed as uncaring and willing to use censorship to protect itself. Good employee relations would have ensured that staff were told in a dignified manner by senior management and given an internal forum to freely express their feelings.

See also

Q10   Why should I use PR to communicate effectively with staff?

Q11   What are the main tools of internal communications?

Q10   Why should I use PR to communicate with staff?

Internal PR is aimed at employees, contractors and volunteers. All too often, organisations boast that their greatest asset is their staff, yet fail to treat them as the important public that they are.

Changes in workplaces over the last few decades have created an environment where open communication with employees is crucial:

- Authoritarian communication from the top down is seen as outdated, patronising and ineffective;
- The 'job for life' has given way to increased employee mobility;
- The regulatory environment places more responsibility on organisations to act transparently in employee affairs;
- The workplace has been democratised, with worker-directors, management-buy-outs and employee shareholding incentives changing the nature of internal relationships.

Internal PR fulfils a number of strategic purposes by:

- Building support for new initiatives and change;
- Achieving staff buy-in to your organisation's mission, vision and values;
- Motivating employees;
- Encouraging feedback;
- Attracting and inducting new employees, and reducing staff turnover;
- Creating a workforce that can relate to external publics;
- Counteracting rumour and gossip during crises, or change.

It also helps your organisation to understand different types of employees, and devise more effective ways of communicating with them:

- **Unguided missiles:** Employees who do not know your strategic direction, but are determined to help anyway;

- **Hot shots:** Committed and dynamic, with a full appreciation of your strategy and their role in it;
- **Slow burners:** Lacking interest in their work and your organisation;
- **Refuseniks:** Understand your strategy, but are resistant to any change that threatens their professional standing or duties.

See also
Q9   How do PR and human resource management complement each other?
Q11   What are the main tools of internal communications?

Q11 What are the main tools of internal communications?

There are a number of channels that can be used to communicate with staff:

- Internal newsletter or magazine, in printed or electronic versions;
- Intranet;
- Annual report and policy documents;
- Noticeboards;
- Email.

While these ensure that communication goes out, staff may not be actively scanning noticeboards, or looking forward to the next issue of the company newsletter. Encourage staff to submit notices, articles, letters or photographs for inclusion; this creates a sense of ownership, increases interest, and prevents the channels being seen as a way for management to lecture staff.

Other channels encourage more interaction between management and staff:

- Briefing sessions;
- Training workshops;
- Internal conferences;
- Question and answer sessions.

Suggestion boxes may be a little old-fashioned but, used properly, can harness employee creativity. Employees should be given due recognition when suggestions are adopted.

Recognising their professional and personal achievements also can motivate employees, and make otherwise dull forms of internal communication more interesting and relevant.

The effectiveness of management walkabouts cannot be over-emphasised. When employees see managers regularly and have the opportunity to interact with them, it fosters more open communication.

Informal channels such as social events, sports or cultural activities are also useful. A five-a-side football competition between departments or a staff talent show can create a sense of belonging and competiveness.

See also

Q9   How do PR and human resource management complement each other?

Q10   Why should I use PR to communicate effectively with staff?

Q60   What content should go in a newsletter or e-zine?

Q12 What is the difference between PR and marketing?

Marketing informs customers about a product or service and persuades them to buy it. This definition emphasises a transaction, and was a popular depiction of marketing until marketers saw that relationships also were important. However, while marketing relationships focus on repeat purchasing, PR builds trust, goodwill and dialogue.

Marketing is concerned with all aspects of the product or service, from research and development, production, pricing, packaging, distribution, promotion to after-sales service. It has little involvement in activities away from the marketplace, such as investor relations, community relations, lobbying, crisis management and internal communications, which are PR activities.

Many marketers see PR as a promotional element of marketing, and do not appreciate its wider uses, or its ability to communicate with publics more effectively than marketing. No business, for example, can fight a crisis using special offers, or rely on corporate branding to satisfy the information needs of investors and shareholders.

How results are measured also differs. PR results are often intangible, dealing in opinions and behaviour, while marketing uses sales figures, profits and market share to show results.

There is, however, an overlap between PR and marketing. Promotions, sponsorships, celebrity endorsements and branding may be carried out by marketing or public relations professionals, or both. A new hybrid called 'marketing public relations' or 'consumer PR' manages the promotion, branding and reputation of products and services.

See also
Q13   What is integrated marketing communication?
Q14   What does PR do for brands that advertising and marketing do not?
Q15   How do I manage sponsorship effectively?
Q16   What will celebrity endorsements do for my organisation?

Q13   What is integrated marketing communication?

Integrated marketing communication (IMC) describes a process of communicating with customers using:

- PR;
- Marketing;
- Advertising;
- Sales promotion;
- Direct mail;
- Social media.

By integrating these into one strategy, your organisation knows that publics and customers receive the same message all the time. IMC starts a dialogue with customers that builds brands, helps sales, and takes place across print and broadcast media, online and outdoor advertising channels.

IMC grew as companies realised that a marketing relationship based on selling and buying needed to develop long-term communication to win customer loyalty and to build the company and brand reputation.

Using IMC successfully needs:

- A **customer database** showing demographic, psychographic and behavioural information;
- A **communications strategy** that identifies the core message and marketing objectives, and relevant publics and markets;
- A **tactical programme** using various communication techniques to reach the target audience;
- **Evaluation of the programme** to identify what worked well and what needs to be changed in future campaigns.

See also
Q12   What is the difference between PR and marketing?

Q14 What does PR do for brands that advertising and marketing do not?
Q15 How do I manage sponsorship effectively?
Q16 What will celebrity endorsements do for my organisation?

Q14   What does PR do for brands that advertising and marketing do not?

A brand is a name, a logo or a design that distinguishes one product, or company, from another. It also brings added value to the product. Marketing, advertising and PR are very powerful – and use different techniques – in helping brands stand out.

Marketing uses a variety of techniques, including packaging and positioning a product in the marketplace, to build brand awareness and generate sales. Marketing is used also to build brand equity, which is the power and financial value of a brand.

Advertising uses persuasive mass media communications to make consumers aware of brands, and to inspire trial or repeat purchases. This communication is one-way and does not create a dialogue. Indeed, consumers, who are exposed to hundreds of advertisements daily, may be unaware of many, or actively avoid them. Advertising has a brand maintenance function, as it works best at reinforcing messages received by consumers.

Both marketing and advertising are concerned with generating sales of a product and service.

PR has a brand-building role, especially for new products, as it establishes the dialogue between your organisation and publics that creates goodwill and trust. It is not directly involved in generating sales: instead, it informs publics about positive aspects of your brand and organisation's identity.

It is very useful in building your organisation's reputation, which can be used to defend a brand should it encounter crises like a product recall.

Because PR efforts are sometimes reported as news by the media, it has higher credibility than advertising. They also may be better targeted than advertising.

See also
Q12   What is the difference between PR and marketing?

Q13   What is integrated marketing communication?
Q15   How do I manage sponsorship effectively?
Q16   What will celebrity endorsements do for my organisation?

Q15   How do I manage sponsorship effectively?

If you want to use sponsorship, begin by considering your objectives:

- Promote your organisation or a product;
- Generate publicity;
- Support marketing, advertising and sales efforts;
- Reach out to a new or wider audience;
- Build community relations.

Next, consider the publics with whom you wish to communicate. Where are they to be found? What are their interests? What messages should they receive? Most sponsorships take place in one of five environments, which together reach out to practically every public:

- Sport;
- Arts and culture;
- Social causes;
- Education;
- Television.

Setting a budget is next. Promoting and managing your involvement will cost two to three times more than you give in sponsorship. Plan in detail how you will spend this supporting investment.

Selecting the right sponsorship is crucial. It should be consistent with your organisation's values – a vodka brand sponsoring an underage sports tournament would be a poor fit. Examine a shortlist of sponsorship opportunities. Are they one-off events, or long-term prospects? Who organises them? What is their reputation? Would your organisation be a replacement for an existing sponsor, or one of many?

Planning your organisation's involvement acknowledges that sponsorship is more than just donating money. It should result in you and the sponsored party working for mutual benefit. Will your employees be involved, officially or as volunteers? Will you offer corporate hospitality to clients? How will your sponsorship be visible to your publics?

When the sponsorship has been implemented, you should evaluate your involvement to see whether objectives were met in a cost-effective way before renewing the sponsorship.

See also

Q12   What is the difference between PR and marketing?
Q13   What is integrated marketing communication?
Q14   What does PR do for brands that advertising and marketing do not?
Q16   What will celebrity endorsements do for my organisation?

Q16　What will celebrity endorsements do for my organisation?

The idea of a celebrity endorsement is to use somebody's fame to draw attention to a product or service. The celebrity may agree to endorse an organisation:

- For payment;
- Because it helps to build their reputation;
- Because they believe that your organisation does good work.

Most endorsements occur in the fashion, cosmetics, technology, consumer goods and charity sectors. The typical celebrity is a sports star, musician, actor, media presenter or – increasingly with reality television shows – somebody famous for being famous. In the UK, members of the royal family lend patronage to worthy causes, which is a type of celebrity endorsement.

Your organisation gains from the 'halo effect' – the celebrity's name and fame reflects on you and creates awareness of what you do or offer. This can help to:

- Build your brand;
- Build reputation;
- Communicate with key publics;
- Increase sales;
- Raise awareness and, for charities, encourage donations.

Endorsements can benefit your organisation and the celebrity, and a long-running partnership can emerge.

However, endorsements also can backfire. A sports star who fails a drugs test, an actor caught drunk driving, or a personality who tweets an inappropriate comment can attract negative publicity. You will need to act swiftly to protect your organisation, and may have to sack the celebrity.

It is important to make sure that the celebrity is not over-exposed. In small media markets like Ireland, a handful of popular celebrities endorse several organisations, arguably diluting their value to each one.

See also
Q12   What is the difference between PR and marketing?
Q13   What is integrated marketing communication?
Q14   What does PR do for brands that advertising and marketing do not?
Q15   How do I manage sponsorship effectively?

Q17   What events are good for promotion and publicity?

Generally speaking, when choosing what kind of event to use for promotion and publicity, your choice will be events that you organise or events organised by another organisation.

Internally-organised events usually target the media, though some include shareholders and potential clients. They include:

- Press conferences;
- Press briefings;
- Photo calls;
- Facility visits;
- Open days;
- AGMs.

Events aimed at your employees are also important. Special or regular events can create a good atmosphere for employees, and increase your reputation when it comes to recruitment – for example:

- Social outings – leisure, cultural, sporting;
- Team-building seminars and activity days;
- Celebrations of anniversaries and successes;
- Annual parties at Christmas or a summer barbecue.

If your organisation is involved in manufacturing products or providing a service, there are several types of event to choose from:

- Exhibitions;
- Trade fairs;
- Workshops;
- Conferences;
- Seminars.

Finally, if your organisation is a not-for-profit or charity, you may want to consider events that combine promotion with advocacy or fundraising – for example:

- Charity auctions;
- Charity balls;
- Endurance events, like sponsored cycles, bed pushes, or fun runs;
- Participatory events, where volunteers come together for a particular purpose; these are popular with environmental groups that organise clean-ups of parks and rivers, or NGOs that build housing and infrastructure in the developing world.

It is always worth seeing what other organisations do for promotion and publicity. Being creative gets attention, but a simple, well-run event is always better than a clever flop.

See also
Q2 What can PR do for my organisation?
Q18 What is a pseudo-event?

Q18   What is a pseudo-event?

A pseudo-event is a special event organised to attract attention. However, the apparent purpose of the event is not the real motivation for organising it. Instead, there is an underlying message that, in itself, may not be very newsworthy but that your organisation would like to have known.

The term is usually used in a negative way, but that is not entirely fair. Identifying a newsworthy angle for an issue is part and parcel of everyday PR. Indeed, some important issues would not receive any media coverage were it not for a pseudo-event taking place – for example:

- A protest rally outside the national parliament seeking state support for sufferers of a rare genetic condition will get media coverage, when the issue itself is much too obscure. But the event brings the issue to public attention;

- A politician using the opportunity of a visit to a school to announce a minor change in state funding of school sports facilities;

- A multi-national company creating a modest number of jobs would receive equally modest coverage, but a facility visit with the group CEO could increase the newsworthiness of the expansion.

Good pseudo-events match the real news story with an appropriate event to highlight. They should never use a deliberately misleading combination of event and news story, or bury a bad news story within an event, as the damage to reputation and relationships could be long-lasting.

See also
Q17   What events are good for promotion and publicity?
Q19   Are publicity stunts useful?
Q84   What is astroturfing?

Q19   Are publicity stunts useful?

Publicity stunts can be a great way of attracting attention to your product, service or organisation. They can add real news value to what you want to say, and can result in increased awareness and support.

Stunts can come in many guises:

- Fun and quirky world record attempts;
- Feats of skill;
- Door-stepping politicians to promote a lobby campaign;
- Smart mobs – a variation of flash mobs, where people use social media to arrange assembling in an area to engage in a short, often pointless, activity, then disperse. Traditional flash mobs are non-commercial, but smart mobs can be used for commercial promotion, or to highlight a lobby issue.

Whatever kind of stunt you organise, it must highlight your message. Otherwise the stunt will be remembered, but what you had to say will not.

Remember, too, that the stunt should work as planned, and cause no harm. LG Electronics was forced to end a stunt in Korea after several people were hospitalised. The firm attached vouchers for its new G2 smart phone to 100 helium balloons, but – not unreasonably – failed to anticipate that people would use BB guns and homemade spears to land one of the prizes. As well as it being a disastrous launch, LG also ended up paying medical costs of those injured.

> **In Practice**
>
> Suicide and self-harm are sensitive subjects, but a publicity stunt organised by volunteers in an Irish town to raise awareness and funds for the Pieta House charity used humour cleverly, and, most importantly, inoffensively. The stunt attempted to set a record for the most people dressed as nuns in a single area for the *Guinness Book of Records*. Over 1,400 people took part in the attempt in Listowel, Co. Kerry, breaking the previous record by around 1,100, and creating a huge amount of positive publicity for the charity.

See also

Q17   What events are good for promotion and publicity?
Q18   What is a pseudo-event?

Q20   What is controlled media?

Controlled media is any form of communication produced by your organisation and delivered directly to your intended publics.

Your organisation has complete control over the content, tone, style, design, placement and timing of the communication. It is able to ensure that the integrity of the message – what you have to say and how you say it – is not altered by anybody.

In this, it differs from mediated communication, which is sent to a third party – like a journalist – who can decide to make the communication known in its entirety, in abridged form, or in an editorialised way.

Most commonly, controlled media include:

- Newsletters;
- Brochures;
- Factsheets;
- Annual reports;
- Podcasts;
- Blogs;
- Corporate videos;
- Your organisation's website and intranet;
- E-mails.

Social media is often mistakenly assumed to be a form of controlled media. However, the degree of interactivity with publics, which includes their comments on blogs or podcasts, retweets and so on, means that some form of editorialising or mediation is carried on by the publics themselves.

Some forms of communication can be both controlled and mediated, depending on their usage. A press release or captioned photograph intended for a newspaper, for example, becomes controlled media when your organisation publishes them on your website.

See also

Q60   What content should go in a newsletter or e-zine?

Q21 What is financial PR?

Financial PR builds awareness of a commercial organisation among influential bodies in the financial marketplace, with the purpose of influencing investors and shareholders through them.

It is used also to communicate with the financial marketplace in relation to specific activities:

- Acquisitions and mergers;
- Take-overs;
- Initial public offers (IPOs) / flotations on stock exchanges;
- New share issues;
- Voluntary de-listing from stock exchanges;
- Interim (figures for part of the trading year) and annual results;
- News that contains price-sensitive information – that is, information that affects the share price.

Specifically, financial PR focuses on relationships with:

- Banks, pension brokers, insurance companies and other financial institutions;
- Financial and industry regulators;
- Governments and international trade organisations;
- Stock exchanges and stockbrokers;
- Investment analysts and rating agencies;
- Financial media.

Shareholders and other investors (venture and angel capitalists, and institutional buyers) are usually communicated with through investor relations programmes, which are part of the financial PR strategy.

The most common tool to communicate with financial publics is the annual report, which combines financial information with insights into future strategies. The report is usually launched at an annual general meeting (AGM) where the directors have the opportunity to listen to shareholders.

Media relations plays a role, too, with press briefings, interviews with senior management and announcements to the market *via* press releases being the most common interactions.

Regulations and legislation dictate what kind of information may be communicated. The financial PR manager must obey all legal obligations to avoid criminal acts such as insider trading, or interfering with the operation of the market by artificially adjusting share prices. Even the appearance of non-compliance can damage your organisation's reputation.

See also
Q6   What is relationship management?

Q22 What is litigation PR?

Litigation PR is a specialised form of reputation management, used when your organisation is involved in a legal action, or a public inquiry. These proceedings can extend over lengthy periods of time, often years, and can cause serious damage to your organisation's reputation, whether you are involved as a defendant, plaintiff, or simply a witness.

Organisations can find themselves in court for many reasons:

- Civil action taken by a client, supplier, employee or other public;
- Civil action for breach of copyright, patent or contract;
- Civil or criminal action after a crisis;
- Criminal action for insider trading, corruption, negligence or corporate homicide;
- Summonsed as a witness to a government inquiry or tribunal.

Frequently, litigation PR is busiest when your case is not before the courts, as this is when you have most opportunity to plead your case in the court of public opinion. Once hearings commence, you must manage communications without interfering with the legal process, which may be illegal or in contempt of court. Your PR should be done in consultation with your legal counsel to ensure that communications are factually and legally sound.

Litigation PR:

- Makes your point of view known and understood;
- Makes complicated issues, such as financial or patent law, understandable to the media and public;
- Provides media with information to ensure balanced coverage;
- Counters negative publicity from other parties to the action, media and rivals;
- Communicates directly with employees and other stakeholders.

In Practice

Even when you win a legal action, your reputation may suffer. The 'McLibel' case in the UK, where McDonalds defended itself against libellous comments by environmental activists, won the company few admirers during the 10 years of hearings: much media commentary was sympathetic towards the defendants and portrayed them as David *versus* Goliath. Although McDonalds won £40,000 in damages, which it declined to collect from the defendants, the damage to its reputation was already too significant to be repaired by the gesture.

See also

Q7   What is reputation management?

Q8   How do I manage reputation?

Q23   What is community PR?

Sometimes called community relations, community PR involves managing your organisation's relationship with probably its most diverse public: the local community. Apart from living close to where your organisation is based, members of the community may have little in common. They may differ in their lifestyle, behaviour, demographic profile and more. Some may be members of local organisations like residents' associations, chambers of commerce or activist groups that interact directly with your organisation. Clearly, reaching out to such a broad group is not easy.

However, your organisation is an important part of the community, and has an obligation to that community to conduct itself in a manner that benefits everybody.

You also have strategic reasons for wanting to maintain good community relations:

- Creating a dialogue to allow the community and your organisation to discuss mutual concerns;
- Promoting your organisation as a socially-responsible member of the community;
- Building goodwill in the community to enhance recruitment;
- Supporting community development to demonstrate your commitment to the community;
- Supporting employee participation in community groups and events.

Communities can be reached through:

- Sponsorships of events and organisations;
- Community forums, where your organisation and members of the community meet publicly to discuss issues of common interest;
- Social events, such as family days, open days and visits by schools, hosted by your organisation;
- Making facilities and employees available for events;

Community relations need to be carried out with vigilance to ensure that your organisation does not divide the community through its actions. A decision to build an annex to a factory may be met with approval by locals who see job creation as important, and disapproval by those concerned that it will cause pollution. Diplomacy is needed to maintain a balance.

HINT

If your organisation has a set budget for a community relations programme, it could ask employees to decide how a portion of it could be spent. If they live locally, their ideas may resonate more with the community than ideas thought of by management.

See also
Q6   What is relationship management?

Q24   I need to write a PR plan – is there a model I can follow?

A PR plan can be a simple one-off event or activity, such as a photo call, or a comprehensive 12-month schedule of sustained activity tied into the organisation's strategic objectives.

Both use the same planning template. The only difference is the length and detail involved. Below is a simple template that will help maintain a focus on each step of the plan.

Sections of the plan	What to include
Executive Summary	A brief outline of the purpose behind the plan, what it is intended to do, the total budget available, and a timeframe for implementing it.
Situation Analysis	What are the issues? Who are the publics? What are their opinions? Do opinions need to be changed or re-affirmed? What is the state of the internal and external environments?
Objectives	State two or three desired objectives that address each issue fully. Each objective should be SMART: specific, measurable, achievable, relevant and time-bound.
Key publics	Prioritise the publics affected by each issue. What media channels are best to communicate with them?
Core messages	Pick two or three messages that relate to all the issues. State why they are important, and what response is desired from publics.
Strategies	This is the big picture part of the plan, based on moving the organisation from where it is, to where it wants to be. Clearly described strategies will improve tactical planning.

Sections of the plan	What to include
Tactics	Itemise the specific tasks that will address each issue and achieve the objectives set. Detail the issue, publics, activities, selected media, dates, costs and resources relevant to each tactic.
Evaluation	Have objectives been met? Outline measurement techniques for media coverage. Outline what external evaluation will be needed – for example, focus groups or market research. Show how the results of evaluation will feed into future plans.

See also

Q25 Where can I find PR campaign case studies, just to give me some ideas?

Q29 I'm just not very creative – will my PR efforts suffer?

Q25 Where can I find PR campaign case studies, just to give me some ideas?

Getting hold of good PR case studies can be tricky. College textbooks provide examples but, with one eye on teaching theory, they are generally of limited use if you want practical guidance.

PR consultancies sometimes post short snapshots of campaigns on their websites, and a quick Internet search can throw up some interesting results. While such case studies may give a reasonable understanding of how a consultancy represented a client, remember that they are written as part of the consultancy's sales pitch to future clients and staff.

The Public Relations Consultants' Association (PRCA) presents annual PR Excellence awards for Irish campaigns in consumer, business to business, media relations, charity, budget and other categories. It publishes case studies of winning entries written by the consultants themselves. These are quite short (around four to six pages) and offer some insights into how a PR professional approaches the planning and implementation of a campaign. PR Excellence case studies for several years may be found at **www.prca.ie**.

The Chartered Institute of Public Relations in the UK runs a similar awards programme and publishes winning case studies on its website for members of the institute. The institute offers reasonable rates for overseas membership for non-practitioners, however. Case studies can be found at **www.cipr.co.uk/content/policy-resources/case-studies**.

In America, the Arthur W Page Association, named after a pioneer in the development of professional public relations, awards an annual prize for a student case study. Though they are academic, the case studies are excellent examples of public relations in practice. They can be read at **www.awpagesociety.com/insights/winning-case-studies/**.

See also
Q24   I need to write a PR plan – is there a model I can follow?
Q29   I'm just not very creative – will my PR efforts suffer?

Q26   How do I carry out a situation analysis?

A situation analysis is the starting point of a PR campaign. It helps your organisation to define itself, and how it interacts with its internal and external environment. While giving a snapshot of where your organisation is at a point in time, it also identifies issues, publics and trends.

There are two commonly used tools for carrying out a situation analysis: SWOT and PESTLE. A communications audit may be seen as a third, though it also could be part of the others.

A SWOT (Strengths, Weaknesses, Opportunities and Threats) analysis is an inward-looking tool that examines the internal environment. It is often drawn as a simple four-box grid, but this does not do justice to the amount of research that is needed.

Strengths – e.g. Resources (assets, people, financial). Competitive advantage (innovation, processes). Culture (management, knowledge).	Weaknesses – e.g. Resources (financial, people). Management (no vision, staff turnover). Competitive weakness (market reach, rivals).
Opportunities – e.g. Markets (expansion, new, niche, high demand). Trends (lifestyle, behavioural, industry). Partnerships (alliances, joint ventures).	Threats – e.g. Economics (boom-bust cycle, high demand). Political and legislative effects (laws, policy). Competitors (new entrants, price wars).

The lists vary with organisations. Some weaknesses can be strengths, some opportunities threats, and *vice versa*. A SWOT matrix uses the combinations SW, SO, ST, WO, WT, OT to determine a strategic direction for the organisation.

A PESTLE (Political, Economic, Social, Technological, Legal and Environmental) analysis is an outward-looking tool that examines your organisation's external environment. It can include:

- **Political:** Proposed legislation, change of governments and policies, political stability;
- **Economic:** Growth or recession, costs of doing business, access to finance;
- **Social:** Population trends, attitudes, values and behaviours, level of education;
- **Technological:** New advances and obsolescence, investment, changing work practices;
- **Legal:** Government regulations and laws, patent wars, data protection;
- **Environmental:** Ethics, green environment, fair trade, social responsibility.

PESTLE is a very useful tool to use in boundary spanning and issues management.

HINT	If you find it hard to distinguish between micro and macro external environments, think of your organisation as being at the centre of two concentric circles – the *Inner* of the two starts with I (so micro) while the circle *Around* everything starts with A (macro).

See also

Q27 What is boundary spanning in PR?
Q90 What is an issue?
Q91 What is issues management?

Q27   What is boundary spanning in PR?

Boundary spanning is a form of environmental scanning that helps your organisation to better understand its external publics and issues. It helps management know how to build stronger relationships with those publics to address the issues.

PR has a unique position within organisations: it operates on the very edge of the organisation, and practitioners are in frequent contact with external publics. As a result, their role looks both inwards and outwards. This gives them the ability to:

- Interact with external publics;
- Assess the likely impact of the organisation's actions on the publics;
- Hear what those publics have to say, and understand how they perceive the organisation;
- Report to management with that information and advice on how to respond.

This makes the PR practitioner an 'honest broker' who mediates between your organisation and its publics. It makes their input into strategic planning very worthwhile. In particular, boundary spanning is essential to issues management. The function gives early warning of future dangers and opportunities, and allows ample time to address them.

See also
Q26   How do I carry out a situation analysis?
Q90   What is an issue?
Q91   What is issues management?

Q28 How do I evaluate my PR efforts?

Evaluation is a difficult aspect of PR. Unlike advertising or marketing, which can use sales figures or market share, PR results like goodwill and behavioural change are often intangible.

The most widely used measurement technique is the Advertising Value Equivalent (AVE). This multiplies the column inches or airplay a campaign receives by the advertising cost of the space it occupied. It produces a notional value, but does not consider how many people read or heard the story, or whether it was covered positively or negatively. AVE is unsuitable for evaluating Internet coverage on blogs and forums that do not carry advertisements.

A similar technique is based on Opportunities to See (OTS). The Joint National Readership Survey in Ireland (JNRS) and the Audit Bureau of Circulation (ABC) in the UK verify sales and readership figures of newspapers and magazines. An item on the front page of a national tabloid newspaper has a higher rating than the same story on an inside page of a broadsheet. Again, this does not evaluate how the story was covered, or how many people read it.

A more sophisticated approach measures:

Stage	What happens	What to measure
Inputs	Press releases are written, photo-calls, contacting media and follow-ups, etc.	Time spent researching and writing material, and contacting media.
Outputs	The press release and photo call are covered by the media.	Who covered the press release? Who read, watched or listened to it? How was it covered in social media outlets?

Stage	What happens	What to measure
Outcomes	The campaign has an effect.	Change in awareness of target publics. Behavioural change in these publics. Attitude change in these publics.

PR measurement may need to spend as much on research as on a campaign itself. Evaluating goodwill may require analysing data from surveys and focus groups. This is time-consuming and expensive but can measure precisely the effectiveness of a campaign. A communication audit can measure the effectiveness of your PR activities over a longer period.

HINT	The Chartered Institute of Public Relations (UK) publishes an excellent user-friendly Research, Planning and Measurement Toolkit on its website **www.cipr.co.uk.**

See also
Q77   What is a communications audit?
Q78   How do I carry out a communications audit?

Q29   I'm not very creative – will my PR efforts suffer?

Yes – and no! Creativity is important for planning in PR, but most tactical work, like writing a press release, is routine. Some strategic activities also require little creativity: communication audits and media training are activities best carried out systematically.

For activities that require creativity, use professionals to provide the creative spark: photographers, videographers, web and print designers are used to receiving briefs that set strategies, but need a creative input to achieve outcomes.

Every public relations practitioner has to be creative at some point, however. The good news is that creativity is innate to everybody, and can be developed by using a few simple techniques until they become second nature:

- **Learn to unlearn:** Modern education focuses on rote learning and answering exam questions by template. Society prefers conformists to rebels. This harms creativity. Unlearn the rules to understand when they are being followed simply because nobody thought to ask 'is there another way?';

- **Use mindmaps:** Big, colourful combinations of words and images help planning, from the content of a press release to a year-long campaign. Because they are so visual, mindmaps allow concepts to emerge more fluidly than bullet points or lists;

- **Think like a child:** Children suspend reality to create an alternate world. For an adult, an empty cardboard box goes in the recycling bin. For a child, it is a spaceship, boat, castle – anything. Examine problems and opportunities with the free-thinking curiosity of a child;

- **Daydream about work tasks:** Jot down ideas that come to mind in a notebook and periodically review the contents;

- **View problems through the eyes of a role model:** Everybody has a mentor or role model to whom they look up, and whose advice they seek. Try exploring problems or opportunities through their eyes: What would they do? How would they do it?

HINT

To build an excellent, creative vocabulary, select three random unknown words each day from the dictionary. Write each and its definition on separate index cards. Use each word three times during the day, then record these uses on the index cards. Your vocabulary will increase by over 1,000 words every year.

See also

Q24   I need to write a PR plan – is there a model I can follow?
Q25   Where can I find PR campaign case studies, just to give me some ideas?

ENGAGING WITH PROFESSIONALS

Q30   How do I build a relationship with journalists?

There is a perception that journalists and press officers have an odd relationship, both needing each other yet neither willing to admit it. The relationship is based on meeting mutual needs, and understanding how the other works. Some people alternate between journalism and public relations, so today's adversary could be tomorrow's colleague.

Professionalism is the best way to build a working relationship with journalists. When you give journalists well-written copy that is newsworthy and factual, you have already created a relationship. Being available to comment on bad news stories can win respect from journalists. Disclosing an interest to a journalist, and being clear about who you represent, helps to show that the relationship is based on honesty and transparency.

Hospitality and token gifts are tricky. While it is fine to offer journalists refreshments at an event, lunches on your organisation's account (even if you and a journalist are friends) are not. An exception is where several journalists are invited to a briefing lunch with a senior manager. Also, while it may be appropriate to send a journalist a token gift at Christmas, this should be done with caution and sensitivity, and not at all if it is likely to offend.

You should understand journalists' roles and needs. They need material to fill column inches and airtime, and to satisfy their audience's need for news. They do not exist to give organisations positive publicity – bad news and criticism can be expected, and should taken in a dignified way. Making journalists fearful is a good device for television comedies like *The Thick of It*, but the reality is that:

- berating journalists for negative coverage;
- holding grudges and blacklisting individuals;
- stonewalling access to spokespersons;
- insisting on seeing interview questions in advance, or

- insisting that you give final approval to a piece before publication or broadcast

will not endear you to them. Yet all are done, and still the press officers who do them wonder why they do not enjoy the same relationship with journalists as their peers.

See also
Q31   How do I decide what media to contact with a press release?
Q32   Are alternative media a bit *too* alternative for my needs?

Q31   How do I decide what media to contact with a press release?

There are services available that distribute press releases on behalf of an organisation to a large list of media contacts. This can be useful for small organisations, where the PR work is the responsibility of an owner-manager, or there is a lack of knowledge of how media relations works. These services may suit some organisations, but a properly targeted press release is usually more effective.

Picking the right media can be done by asking a few basic questions:

- What is the purpose of the press release – is it about a product launch, lobby campaign, or merger, for example? Is it suitable for business, trade, consumer or lifestyle media?
- What publics are being targeted?
- What media reach most of these publics? Are they relevant to these publics?
- Which of these media have the highest credibility with the target publics?
- Have any of these media accepted or ignored previous press releases? What is your organisation's relationship with each media outlet and its staff?
- Which of these media are most cost-effective? Some may require longer lead-in time, or more information, which will add to time costs for an in-house press office, or increase the hourly bill from a consultancy;
- Which of these media will get the message out on time?

While there is no guarantee that the media will use a press release, the better you understand your organisation's publics and their media use, the better able you are to ensure that journalists receive relevant press releases.

See also

Q30   How do I build a relationship with journalists?
Q32   Are alternative media a bit *too* alternative for my needs?

Q32 Are alternative media a bit *too* alternative for my needs?

It all depends what is meant by alternative media. It is common to think of anything outside the mainstream media as alternative – youth-orientated, politically radical and counter-cultural media especially – and perhaps a little fanatical.

In fact, alternative media incorporate a range of interests, from minority sports, music, film, human rights, politics, environment, to health and many more. They include newspapers, magazines, blogs, Internet forums, television and radio programmes, and even dedicated channels. Their audiences may be very diverse, and quite mainstream: a football fanzine like *When Saturday Comes* could be avidly read by a middle-aged accountant, for instance.

Press officers might be surprised to realise that the magazine *Simply Knitting* had an audited average circulation in the UK of over 40,000 in 2012, or that three golf magazines averaged around 150,000 in total in the same period. Few would regard knitting and golf as alternative lifestyles, but – aside from sports coverage of golf tournaments – neither receives much attention from the traditional mainstream media.

Alternative media offer direct access to publics whose interests are clearly identifiable, and who can be reached through a small number of publications and broadcasts. However, their editorial line can be very severe: because they see themselves as championing a particular interest or point of view, they can be dogmatic and polarising. This is true of many religious and political alternative media. Any negative fallout from their coverage should be considered before you make contact with them.

See also
Q31 How do I decide what media to contact with a press release?
Q33 How do I pitch a story to the media?
Q34 How does a journalist decide what is news?

Q33 How do I pitch a story to the media?

Most times, a press officer looking for media coverage sends out a press release. Occasionally, though, the press officer may have an idea for a feature article – a human interest piece about the new CEO, or a significant anniversary of the organisation, for example. Journalists can be sceptical about accepting material that could be cheap publicity for an organisation, so the press officer must convince them that the article will interest their readers.

Your pitch starts by knowing which editor to talk to. This information can be found in media directories, but these go out of date quickly, so ring the newspaper to confirm a name if you have any doubt. A proposal sent to 'The Editor' may be ignored.

The first contact could be a phone call to an editor, asking whether they are the person to talk to about the idea. This achieves two things: it finds the right person, and initiates personal contact.

Remember that newspapers have different sections, all with their own editor. These include: features, opinion, lifestyle, business, motoring, health, education, entertainment, agriculture and more. Going to a specific editor gives your pitch a better chance of being heard. Sometimes, if they are specialised correspondents, it may be appropriate to pitch directly to journalists.

Once you have an opportunity to pitch, send a short, precise e-mail that includes:

- An outline of the story. An idea is not enough. Who or what is it about? How will it be written? What angle and tone will be used?
- What makes it interesting? Knowing how journalists decide what is newsworthy will help;
- How will it benefit the newspaper to publish it?
- How long will it be?
- Who will write it: you, a staff journalist or a freelancer?
- When will it be ready?

- What photographs could accompany it?

Be alert to basic mistakes that will result in rejection:

- Focussing only on your organisation and how it benefits;

- Being unclear or taking too long to make the point;

- Anything that suggests the pitch has been made before, or to everybody in your contacts book.

See also

Q30   How do I build a relationship with journalists?

Q31   How do I decide what media to contact with a press release?

Q32   Are alternative media a bit *too* alternative for my needs?

Q34   How does a journalist decide what is news?

Q35   What timeframe should I consider for sending material to the media?

Q37   Why won't a journalist accept my press kit and free samples?

Q38   What does on the record, off the record, and non-attributable mean?

Q34 How does a journalist decide what is news?

PR practitioners are likely to divide news into two categories – hard news and soft news.

Hard news deals with events as they are happening, and can include coverage of crises, press conferences, and so on. They are sometimes seen as challenging stories that require instant responses to probing media questions.

Soft news deals with feature articles in areas such as entertainment, the arts, charity campaigns, or profiles of prominent businesspeople, for example. They can be planned and written over a longer period of time than hard news.

Journalists have guidelines for deciding whether something is newsworthy. In the 1960s, two Swedish sociologists, Galtung and Ruge, placed news values in three categories:

- Impact of the news on the audience;
- Identifying the audience;
- Determining how news could be covered.

They produced a list of 12 key words, including

- **Negativity:** Bad news is better than good news;
- **Proximity:** How close the story is to the audience.
- **Currency:** News can run over a period of time – for example, a major industrial crisis may run for over a week and still be considered newsworthy;
- **Uniqueness:** News should be unusual. Most product launches are not unique, unless, like the first mobile phone in 1973, the product has the potential to change society;
- **Personality:** Does the story centre on a high profile individual? Has it a human interest angle?

- **Threshold:** The bigger the impact of a story, the more people that are affected, or the more money it involves, the higher its news value.

Over time, other values have been added to the original list. These include celebrity, meaningfulness and media competition.

See also

Q30   How do I build a relationship with journalists?
Q31   How do I decide what media to contact with a press release?
Q32   Are alternative media a bit *too* alternative for my needs?
Q33   How do I pitch a story to the media?
Q35   What timeframe should I consider for sending material to the media?
Q37   Why won't a journalist accept my press kit and free samples?
Q38   What does on the record, off the record, and non-attributable mean?

Q35 What timeframe should I consider for sending material to the media?

Media outlets work to different deadlines, so you should know the submission requirements of daily, weekly, fortnightly, monthly, bi-monthly, quarterly, bi-annual and annual publications and broadcasts. The purpose of a timeframe is to ensure the most favourable time for coverage. Good planning can ensure that a story intended for the morning newspapers is not so well covered by the television news the night before that no newspaper covers it.

Because print media fit features and soft news into their editions first, saving the most important space for hard and breaking news, it is better to send publicity material to them as early in the editorial cycle as possible.

Media	Time needed for submissions
Glossy magazines (fashion, food, lifestyle) Bi-monthlies, bi-annuals and annuals	Up to several months for artwork and copy.
Weekly local newspaper	Up to the day of printing. Submitting on the day after the paper comes out, as work on the next edition starts, may increase the chances of getting material included.
National Sundays	Up to Saturday evening for hard news. For soft news, as early in the week as possible is best. Feature articles should be negotiated several weeks in advance.

Media	Time needed for submissions
National dailies	Morning newspapers are distributed from about 4.30am. Hard news material should be submitted by 10.00pm. Most press conferences and photo-calls are held much earlier, around 10.00 to 11.30am, while the next edition is practically empty. Evening newspapers' first editions usually appear around 11.30am, so material should be submitted the previous evening, unless it is hard news.
Weekly trade press / weekly magazines	Several weeks for feature articles and artwork, and up to the day before printing for hard news.
Daily radio / TV shows	Hourly news bulletins – allow as much of the hour between bulletins as possible. Breaking news will be taken immediately. News programmes plan running orders of material four to five hours before broadcast. Magazine and chat programmes (features and soft news) should be contacted a week or two in advance. Recorded shows may require over a week for material.
Weekly radio / TV shows	Hard news broadcasts may take material up to the final few hours before broadcast, and during the broadcast for breaking news. Magazine and chat programmes may require over a week for material. Recorded shows may require submissions several months in advance.

See also
Q36   What is an embargo?

Q36 What is an embargo?

An embargo is a request to the media on a press release not to publish or broadcast its contents until after a specific date and time. It is often used when a release is sent to several media outlets working to different deadlines. The purpose is to manage how and when a story is reported so that it creates maximum impact.

An embargo should be prominent on the first page of a press release and written in a simple format:

Embargo: 9.00am, Tuesday, 26 May

Embargoes should be used sparingly and only for news that really justifies its use, for example:

- When a stock exchange quoted company releases information that could affect the markets, or whose early release could be a breach of stock exchange regulations;

- When an organisation is announcing the appointment of a new senior executive, it is sensible to ensure that the public announcement is made only after the candidate has tendered their resignation with their previous employer.

Journalists are not obliged to comply with embargoes, and can reveal the contents of the release before the deadline. Depending on the nature of the news, the pressure to report it ahead of rival media outlets may be too tempting for a journalist. However, embargoes are a matter of trust between journalists and PR practitioners: the journalist who frequently breaks embargoes and the practitioner who over-uses them will find it difficult to maintain trust with each other.

See also
Q35   What timeframe should I consider for sending material to the media?

Q37 Why won't a journalist accept my press kit and free samples?

Journalists will rarely refuse a press kit, unless it offers no new information. What complicates a journalist's decision is the offer of free product samples or a service with the press kit, or at any time.

Media organisations have guidelines for staff and freelancers. These make it clear that accepting a sample or service above a token value could compromise a journalist's integrity, unless it is essential to their work. The same applies to any offer of hospitality above normal courtesy.

Irish and British journalists are bound by the National Union of Journalists' code of ethics. The code advises journalists that they should avoid accepting incentives that could influence their reporting. Similar codes are in place in other countries.

There are occasions when a journalist can accept something free:

- Technology journalists may accept the temporary use of a smart phone or tablet computer for trial and reviewing purposes;
- Travel correspondents often go on press trips paid for by airlines, tourism agencies, hotels and so on. They should state in their report that the trip was paid for by one of these bodies;
- Sports journalists covering fixtures should be given a pass allowing them access to the event;
- Music journalists should be given a press pass for concerts and gigs, and a CD or audiofile of an album for reviews;
- Book reviewers receive a copy of the book.

As a rule of thumb, you should consider whether what is being offered is:

- Essential for journalists to do their job;
- Of token value;
- Not transferrable – for example, a concert pass should be for the sole use of a named music correspondent and not left open for use by colleagues, friends or family.

If any doubt lingers, it is best to check the policy of a media organisation in advance.

See also
Q30   How do I build a relationship with journalists?
Q31   How do I decide what media to contact with a press release?
Q33   How do I pitch a story to the media?
Q34   How does a journalist decide what is news?

Q38   What does on the record, off the record, and non-attributable mean?

These are three levels of speaking to journalists, and you should be aware of them when you or a client are being interviewed. It is useful before starting an interview to establish how they will be used, as it is possible to go on and off the record several times.

Always assume that everything said to a journalist is 'on the record' – that is, what you are saying is what you want to be reported. If you have any reservations about how something might be interpreted and reported, it is best not to mention it.

'Off the record' relies on the journalist's discretion. They decide how to use information that has been given. The most useful type of off the record information is background material that will help the journalist to understand a story in its proper context. You should always state when you are going on and off the record during an interview.

'Non-attributable' means the journalist can use information from an interview, but cannot name the source. This produces phrases such as 'A friend of the singer' or 'Sources close to the Government'. In both cases, the information is probably from a PR adviser, but there is an element of deniability to it. This is one of the problems of non-attribution, and why it is often used in:

- Political PR when a politician or party is trying to leak information to test public response; and
- Celebrity PR where the goal is to maintain a high public profile for a celebrity.

Because non-attributable quotations cannot hold anybody to account, they are often used to communicate stories that may be untrue or exaggerated.

See also
Q30   How do I build a relationship with journalists?
Q34   How does a journalist decide what is news?

Q39 How does citizen journalism affect my organisation?

Citizen journalism, also called public or street journalism, is a type of news reporting where members of the public are involved in gathering, reporting and analysing news material, often of a type not covered by the traditional media. They bypass traditional media by using the Internet: blogging, podcasting and social media sites are very suitable to citizen journalism. Monitoring what is being written online is a new concern for many organisations.

Some citizen journalists are an alternative media channel, enabling organisations to communicate with publics. They are respected experts or social thinkers, with a large following, and are very influential. Forging good relationships with them benefits both your organisation and the citizen journalist.

Others may be driven by ideologies that differ to your organisation's. Activists use citizen journalism to publish material that contradicts organisations or exposes bad practices.

Traditional media have fixed deadlines, but citizen journalists are active around the clock. News items like crises, which could not have been seen unless a television crew happened to be nearby, are recorded and posted online as they unfold. This reduces the time you have to respond.

Because newsgathering is expensive, television stations are broadcasting more footage shot by bystanders. Newspapers also link online reports to websites where such footage can be seen.

Citizen journalists may lack the formal training of journalists working for the traditional media, and errors or poor practice may cause problems for your organisation, including:

- **Bias:** Some citizen journalists, whether intentionally or not, give one-sided coverage or opinions that unfairly damage organisations;

- **Libel:** The speed of online information makes it impossible for your organisation to prevent libellous material spreading. Traditional media outlets are advised by libel lawyers, and journalists receive education in libel law; most citizen journalists do not have these essentials. There is also a lack of awareness among many citizen journalists that libel laws apply to their output;

- **Credibility:** A newspaper masthead gives journalists credibility; there is an organisation that will stand over what they have written. Many citizen journalists are anonymous or use pseudonyms, which can reduce their credibility, and make them hard to hold to account.

See also
Q42   What is media monitoring?

Q40   What is a media briefing?

A media briefing is similar to a press conference in that members of the media are invited to attend an event that you are hosting. However, the event is not meant to be broadcast, nor is it used to make a news announcement, and usually what you say is off the record.

Media briefings tend to take place in informal surroundings, sometimes over a working breakfast or lunch. Your organisation may be represented by up to two or three people, including the CEO, chairman, or senior PR manager.

Typically, invitations are issued to editors and senior correspondents rather than all the journalists with whom you usually deal. This is because they set the editorial policy of their media outlets, and can be more influential than journalists.

Media briefings may be organised to:

- Provide background information;
- Introduce a new senior manager or management team;
- Explain your position on a contentious issue – media briefings are commonly used by NGOs and lobby groups campaigning for a cause.
- Establish your credentials as a reliable and trustworthy source;
- Lay the ground for future communication between you and their journalists;
- Establish why the media have been hostile, and turn that hostility to support or a neutral viewpoint. This is especially necessary when you have been targeted for criticism by rivals or pressure groups that the media have accepted as true;
- Communicate technical details about a product or service.

See also
Q38   What does on the record, off the record, and non-attributable mean?
Q43   How do I organise a press conference?

Q41   When could I use narrowcasting instead of broadcasting?

As the name suggests, narrowcasting is the opposite of broadcasting. Instead of transmitting messages to many publics using the most popular television or radio stations, messages are tailored for a specific, smaller audience, reached *via* niche channels. These include special interests cable and satellite television channels, digital and Internet radio stations, and social media sites that allow podcasts and videos.

Narrowcasting is of particular interest online, which has made communication with small groups easier. Organisations now find that publics identify themselves, and express an interest in communicating. Publics typically emerge from:

- Opt-in mailing and text messaging lists;
- Subscriptions to a website or social media site like a YouTube channel;
- Self-selected followers on social media sites like Twitter;
- Accepted requests to befriend on social media sites like Facebook or LinkedIn;
- Staff intranet.

It makes sense for your organisation to focus on the small number of influential bloggers relevant to it, rather than trying to reach their audiences by your own activities. These influencers shape public opinion. By building a relationship with them, you can reach their audiences more efficiently and cost-effectively. Your messages, communicated through a podcast or video, will probably be interpreted by the influencer for their audience, which may be more accepting of them as they now come from a source they trust.

Narrowcasting offers many advantages:

- Messages reach precise publics, who may have identified themselves to the organisation;
- Online narrowcasting creates dialogue;

- Organisations can decide to prevent some publics – for example, rivals – from being able to access their communications;
- Publics may offer information about themselves that help your organisation to tailor its messages more effectively;
- Basic technology to control your own channels of communication online is widely available, easy to use and not expensive.

See also

Q64 How do I prepare for a broadcast interview?
Q71 Why will people want to listen to my podcast?

Q42 What is media monitoring?

Media monitoring is a way of assessing media attitudes towards your organisation. Information is gathered from newspaper and magazine clippings and transcripts of television and radio broadcasts.

Media monitoring measures five important factors:

- What the media is saying about you. In the case of radio phone-in shows and comments on their websites, this includes what they are allowing to be said about you;
- The accuracy of what is being said about you;
- Their attitude – is it critical, supportive or neutral?
- The quality of their coverage – this measures the actual content and context of coverage, the type of media outlet (community radio or national broadsheet, for example) and the position the coverage occupies (whether it is high up or low down in the running order for a television news broadcast, or front page or inside page of a newspaper);
- Media coverage of competitors and rivals.

By monitoring what is being said, you are able to react more quickly to correct inaccurate or unfair coverage.

Monitoring your local media can be done in-house, as there is probably only a handful of newspapers, most of them weekly publications, that you need to review. Radio monitoring is more difficult as it may not be possible to have staff listening to local stations during work hours. However, there are media monitoring agencies that arrange press clippings and transcripts of broadcasts for national, local and international media coverage.

Increasingly, a lot of media monitoring now focuses on the traditional media's online content, and social media as well. This is quite specialised, though there are many software programmes that will track mentions of your organisation online for basic monitoring.

See also

Q39 How does citizen journalism affect my organisation?
Q40 What is a media briefing?

Q43 How do I organise a press conference?

Advance planning helps a press conference run smoothly. Start by choosing a date and time that facilitates the media. Morning is best, as it give journalists time to file copy for evening editions. Avoid dates that clash with major events, especially ones organised by rivals. It is unprofessional, and may even look like a deliberate sabotage attempt.

Next choose a location. Your headquarters, a hotel, or conference centre is usually best, as you need a venue that provides privacy, audio-visual equipment, adequate space and seating, and perhaps refreshments. Sometimes, if you are launching a new product, you may want to be more creative, so a novel venue may be more appropriate, but avoid anything gimmicky. Make sure that the location is accessible for journalists or speakers with limited mobility and for photographers or TV crews with heavy equipment. Book the venue and confirm the booking a week before the press conference.

Send invitations to your contacts list of journalists a week in advance. Follow up with a reminder call a day or two beforehand. Invitations should be short, with details of your organisation, the reason for the event, participants, and location, time and date.

At the press conference, greet journalists and distribute press kits as they arrive. Start on time, and have a facilitator to host proceedings. State at the outset how long the presentations will be, and how much time will be given to questions and answers. Keep the number of speakers and guests to a minimum: too many dilutes your message, while you want to avoid a situation where there are more of them than journalists. Ensure speakers stress the same message. Finish the presentations on time and allow the media to ask questions.

See also
Q40 What is a media briefing?
Q44 How do I organise a photo call?
Q45 How do I organise a facility visit?
Q46 How do I brief a photographer?

Q44 How do I organise a photo call?

As always when dealing with the media, try to select a date and time that suits their schedules.

While you may be able to host the photo call at your headquarters, unless the building is particularly photogenic or essential to the message, you may be better advised to find a different location, or to tie it into an event. If you intend to use a public place or historical site, check whether a local authority or other agency's permission is needed for photography.

Decide whether the shoot will be indoors or outdoors, and have a contingency plan for bad weather. Think whether you will need to hire props, models, or celebrities, and whether it will be an activity shot or posed picture.

Send short invitations with outline details of the photo call to photo editors and freelance photographers a week in advance, and follow up with a reminder about two days before the photo call.

At the photo call, have your own photographer present: firstly, in case no other photographers attend and, secondly, to take the kind of picture that is fine for your social media sites, but not the press. It can be good for internal relations if several employees and managers are photographed, especially if there is a celebrity present. However, these pictures have no news value and take up time that press journalists do not have, so have your own photographer take them afterwards.

The official photographs should only have the two to three people essential to your message. Have your logo visible, but remember that photo editors will probably crop it out of the printed image.

See also
Q43 How do I organise a press conference?
Q45 How do I organise a facility visit?
Q46 How do I brief a photographer?

Q45   How do I organise a facility visit?

A facility visit is a term that covers different uses. All, though, involve a planned media trip to, for example, a:

- Factory or new production facility;
- New headquarters;
- Hotel and leisure centre;
- Tourist attraction;
- Exhibition or trade show.

It also could be a media trip on board a new ferry or cruise ship, or to a car manufacturer's testing circuit.

Facility visits often are held abroad, especially in the tourist industry, and the 'facility' might encompass an entire city or region.

Because they can involve foreign travel and, even domestically, at least one overnight stay, facility visits demand a lot of planning, often months in advance:

- Select dates and prepare an itinerary. Liaise with overseas staff or associates if necessary;
- Provisionally book hotel accommodation, restaurants, catering and transport. Use corporate travel agencies to provisionally book flights. If the trip is outside the country, get local contacts' advice on hotels and restaurants;
- Send invitations to the media;
- Identify which staff need to travel, and what extra staff will be needed. It is good to have one staff member to every six or so journalists. Brief staff on the purpose of the visit and key messages. Prepare press kits;
- Follow-up to confirm which journalists will travel and confirm all provisional bookings;
- Arrange a meeting point for journalists and staff if travel is involved;

- Stick to the itinerary and be available and accessible to journalists during the visit, but allow them their own time for writing notes and copy;

- Follow up with journalists after the visit. Ask them what worked or did not so future trips can be improved. Provide any additional information they may require.

See also
Q40   What is a media briefing?
Q43   How do I organise a press conference?
Q44   How do I organise a photo call?

Q46   How do I brief a photographer?

There are different types of photographer, so when choosing one for a photo shoot, you must be clear about your needs. Some photographers are generalists, and do a wide range of corporate and press photography, while others, like fashion and food photographers, are highly specialised. No matter which type is hired, you will have to provide a detailed brief.

The brief should:

- Explain the purpose of the photographs – what message will they convey?
- Identify who is to be photographed;
- Identify the intended audience;
- Explain their intended use – are they to be printed in the media, in the organisation's annual report, or used online?
- State the budget available for hire of props, models, location shoots and so on;
- State the timeframe and deadlines – photo shoots for the national press need to be arranged for around 11.00am, with photographs supplied within two hours. Photographs for corporate publications or glossy magazines are needed several months in advance;
- State the quality and size of photographs – glossy magazines need very high resolution images, while newspapers can use a little lower. Lowest of all are compressed images for online use and thumbnails emailed to photo editors by prior arrangement so they can choose the images they want;
- Identify who is responsible for distribution – unless you regularly issue to the press, it is better to pay a little extra and use the photographer's own distribution service.

Discuss the photographer's thoughts on hiring models or celebrities against using staff, using child models or children of staff, using props, and shooting on location or in studio. The more thought that goes into the practical side of the photograph early on, the more scope the photographer has for allowing natural creativity to emerge later.

Let the photographers themselves guide you where possible. They are the professionals and probably will be accredited by the Press Photographers' Association of Ireland, the British Press Photographers' Association, or the National Union of Journalists. Trust the photographer to do the job. Their skills and experience of dealing with the press mean they can advise on the particular type of photograph each publication prefers.

See also

Q44 How do I organise a photo call?

Q47 How do I brief a graphic designer for a print publication?

Q48 How do I brief a web designer for a company website?

Q47   How do I brief a graphic designer for a print publication?

Graphic designers have a keen eye not just for layout, colours and images but also for the strategic impact of their designs. How will the target audience respond? Will the design have its intended effect? They mix design practicalities with the subtleties of strategy to produce work that looks deceptively easy, but is the result of planning and creativity.

A designer needs a clear design brief showing that you have thought about the project, and know what you want. Establishing clarity ensures that designers can do their work without having to constantly seek approval or guidance. It also saves you time and money.

Elements of the design brief	What it tells the designer
Corporate profile	What is your story? What aspects do you want highlighted in the design?
Core business	What does your organisation do – make and sell, provide a service, or fundraise for charity, for instance? The requirements of a luxury brand of car are different to those of a charity.
The client's current design	How are your corporate colours and logo being used in other design work? Has it been effective? Will change be needed? If so, what can you point to for inspiration?
Current market situation	Who are your main competitors? What is the state of the market?
What is to be designed	A brochure, annual report, catalogue and so on.

Elements of the design brief	What it tells the designer
Objectives and key message	What will the design achieve? Will it be measurable in sales, market share, or increased awareness among publics? What key message should publics understand? Is this to be produced in an image, or using a tagline?
Target publics	With whom do you want to communicate? Who are they – what are their demographic or lifestyle characteristics? Where are they located? What media do they use?
The schedule and budget	When do you need the finished design? Is it a realistic timeframe, allowing time for consultation, the creative process and physical production? How much are you willing to spend? Will this have an impact on materials and printing processes, for instance?

See also

Q46   How do I brief a photographer?
Q48   How do I brief a web designer for a company website?

Q48   How do I brief a web designer for a company website?

Website design has two elements: the website visitors see (the front end) and the technical, hidden part (the back end). The information for any graphic design project applies to designing the front end, which is the easier part to design, but one that many organisations mistakenly dwell on.

However, in addition to objectives, targets, messages, style, schedule and budget, the designer needs a technical brief for the complex back end design. This incorporates features visitors to the site never see but rely on: searching for products or information in a database, financial transactions, interaction *via* e-mail or forums, and relying on your organisation to keep their data secure.

Elements of the technical brief	What it tells the designer
Information on the old site, if any	What was good and bad? Why is it being redesigned? What features and functionality should be kept? Is most traffic to the site from computers or smart phones?
Purpose of the new site	Is it a corporate brochure site, requiring little back end programming? Is it an e-commerce site, with sales and payments, stock management, searchable database, order tracking and high levels of security? Will it link to the client's social media sites? Is it an intranet for staff use?
Content for the new site	What written copy, images and audio-video files will be needed? Who will be responsible for creating them?
User and staff requirements	Have you asked clients and customers for advice? What do they want from the site? How can this advice be incorporated into the design, and improve their relationship? Have staff been consulted? What processes would they like to see on the website, or intranet?

Elements of the technical brief	What it tells the designer
Technical requirements	Does your organisation own the domain name? Does it need a hosting service? What level of accessibility is required? Should it be designed for smart phones?
Updating, maintenance and support	Who will update content? Do you have the skills and staff to do it? Do you need a content management system, provided by the designer or another party?
Online promotion	The designer will want to know about any promotional activity, and especially online promotions for which they may have responsibility for: search engine optimisation, search engine paid listings, and social media links and management.

See also

Q46   How do I brief a photographer?
Q47   How do I brief a graphic designer for a print publication?

Q49   What is the role of the PR practitioner?

There are many views on the PR practitioner's role, and they differ depending on where they work. Consultancy, in-house and freelance all have different aspects, though they share some common foundations. Descriptions of the PR role range from the under-whelming 'support to the marketing function' to the grandiose 'voice of the organisation's conscience'. The truth is somewhere in between.

At heart, the PR professional is concerned with communication, and that shapes the role in every way, from strategic planning to tactical work.

The role	What it is concerned with
Management and strategy	Devising the overall communications objective and strategy of an organisation or client, and overseeing its execution. Being part of, or directly advising, the senior management team. A holistic view of how the organisation relates to its external environment and publics.
Tactical and operational	Carrying out campaigns and projects using a range of communications techniques and tactics. Creating and maintaining relationships with key publics. Working with external consultants, design agencies and freelancers. Day-to-day administration of the PR department, or client accounts.
Analytical and reflective	Monitoring the external environment for issues that affect relationships with publics. Building an identity that reflects the organisation's values. Focusing on corporate governance, ethical behaviour and corporate social responsibility. Evaluating the results of PR campaigns and projects.

The role	What it is concerned with
Education	Continuing professional development of the individual practitioner. Providing training for other staff and managers, especially media training, crisis management skills and social media management.

Within this framework, two dominant roles emerge:

- The **communications manager**, who works at the most senior level devising policy and strategy and is less involved in tactical work;

- The **communications technician**, whose work is tactical and focussed on carrying out plans devised by more senior managers. They have little role in strategic PR.

See also
Q50   What are the attributes and skills of a PR practitioner?
Q51   Should I hire a PR consultancy or do the job myself?
Q52   Should I consider hiring freelancers to help my PR efforts?

Q50   What are the attributes and skills of a PR practitioner?

Depictions of PR professionals' attributes in popular culture often highlight their physical attractiveness, extrovert personalities and ruthless decisiveness. The reality is more mundane: being a party animal or insensitive to others' feelings are among the profession's least desirable attributes.

Most PR professionals' attributes and skills can be summarised in four areas:

- **Knowledge** typically includes:
  - A qualification in PR or a related field such as journalism or marketing;
  - A general qualification such as an arts degree. However, specialised degrees in nursing, medicine and finance are highly regarded in consultancies focussing on these sectors;
  - A wide range of life experiences;
  - Inquisitiveness and eagerness to constantly learn new knowledge;
  - Literacy, numeracy, creativity and problem-solving skills;
  - Knowledge of corporate governance and ethics.

- **Technical** requires:
  - An ability to manage people, resources and time;
  - Industry-specific skills, both in the PR industry and the industry where the professional works;
  - An ability to think strategically and implement strategy;
  - Understanding of traditional and new media.

- **Communication** focuses on:
  - Written and verbal skills, both in formal presentation and interpersonal settings;
  - Leadership and motivation skills;
  - Networking;
  - Clarity in providing information and giving instructions;

- Clear thinking.
- **Social and personal** includes:
  - Team players who integrate well with others;
  - An ability to work on one's own initiative, and to shoulder responsibility;
  - Integrity and honesty;
  - Personal confidence;
  - Adaptability, especially in consultancy work where clients may range from government departments to high street retailers.

The list, it is fair to say, is endless. Consultancies highlight different things to in-house positions, and in the course of your career, you may find different aspects highlighted from time to time.

See also
Q49   What is the role of the PR practitioner?
Q51   Should I hire a PR consultancy or do the job myself?
Q52   Should I consider hiring freelancers to help my PR efforts?

Q51   Should I hire a PR consultancy or do the job myself?

Many organisations achieve excellent PR results thanks to the efforts of an employee or manager who takes this role on alongside their regular duties. Most not-for-profit organisations and small and medium businesses manage their relationships, publicity, promotion, and so on in-house. There are good reasons why you can carry out PR in-house:

- You are familiar with the organisation, its issues and publics;
- You have experience of managing PR campaigns and events;
- Your work may focus on a limited range of applications – for example, managing your organisation's social media presence, or infrequent press releases – and would not justify hiring consultants;
- It is cost-effective.

However, there are times when it makes sense to look outside the organisation for the specialised offerings of a consultancy:

- The public relations programme may be too complex or time consuming to be handled in-house;
- Your organisation may be too small to justify paying a full-time PR manager. Consultancies charge per hour, on a fee per project, or on a monthly retainer;
- Consultancies, whether full-service or specialist, have skills and experience that can exceed those found in-house, especially in areas such as crisis management and lobbying;
- Consultancies deal regularly with other professionals, such as web designers, film production companies, photographers and market research agencies, and can hire these on your behalf;
- Consultancies may be local offices of international firms, or have international contacts that can represent your organisation in several countries at the same time;

- As outsiders, consultants are more likely to be objective about your organisation.

That said, consultancies also have disadvantages:

- They can create a layer between your organisation and its publics, especially the media;
- They may not fully appreciate your organisation – no matter how comprehensive the briefing they receive, or how closely they work with you;
- Your organisation gets a time allowance from the consultancy, not round the clock communications with publics.

Every organisation is different, with diverse PR needs. The decision on hiring a consultancy depends on the availability of resources, time and skills in-house, and whether the job can be best done by you or consultants. Hiring consultants is not a sign that the PR task is too big for you: even multinational companies, with huge in-house PR divisions, choose to hire consultancies, believing the advantages sometimes outweigh the disadvantages.

See also
Q49   What is the role of the PR practitioner?
Q50   What are the attributes and skills of the PR practitioner?
Q52   Should I consider hiring freelancers to help my PR efforts?

Q52   Should I consider hiring freelancers to help my PR efforts?

Freelancers can be a very effective way of boosting your PR capabilities. They work for themselves, often as sole traders, in a limited range of activities. Because their overheads are low, they usually cost less than hiring a consultancy. However, some have well-established reputations as experts in their field, and you may pay a premium for their services.

PR freelancers can augment staff numbers, or work as specialists hired for specific projects, where their skills, expertise and connections are lacking in your organisation. Typically, this includes lobbyists, political campaign managers, and strategists in complex areas of public relations like investor relations. They also may be specialised writers, providing copy for in-house publications, annual reports, online material and speeches. They usually charge an hourly fee, project fee or retainer.

Freelance journalists can write feature articles and copy for a wide range of corporate publications. Journalists with technical skills in audio and video recording and editing can help create podcasts and online videos. They are also in demand to provide media training to senior managers. Recent trends in journalism have seen the number of staff journalists decrease, and more freelancers are available for short-term PR contracts or writing commissions.

The National Union of Journalists recommends rates of pay for freelancers, but you can expect to pay more than the recommended minimum for experienced journalists.

Other freelancers include graphic designers and web designers who can provide specialised services that are unavailable in-house, either on a project fee basis or as temporary staff.

See also
Q49   What is the role of the PR practitioner?
Q50   What are the attributes and skills of the PR practitioner?
Q51   Should I hire a PR consultancy or do the job myself?

PRACTICAL PR SKILLS

Q53   What do I put into a press kit?

A press kit, or media pack, is information that has been designed specifically for the media. Organisations in specialised sectors such as pharmaceutical, engineering, or financial services, may find that the journalists with whom they most often deal do not have the technical background to appreciate the organisation and its sector. A well-thought-out press kit can address this.

The press kit is sent out to journalists on request, as a mail-shot, or distributed at a press conference. Usually, it contains some or all of:

- A press release;
- Background material with information on products, manufacturing processes, or financial results, for example;
- Copies of speeches made at the press conference;
- Frequently asked questions and answers;
- Photographs for publication;
- Biographies of key individuals;
- Brochures or leaflets;
- Client, consumer or associate testimonials.

Product samples or specimens also may be included. However, they should not have more than a token value as some media outlets may not allow their journalists to accept them otherwise.

Press kits are also called press packs. As this term also refers to groups of journalists competing for stories, often about celebrities or crises, it is best avoided for clarity.

See also
Q37   Why won't a journalist accept my press kit and free samples?`
Q54   What's the secret of a good press release?
Q55   What should I avoid when writing a press release?
Q56   What content goes in a holding statement?
Q73   What is an electronic press kit?

Q54 What's the secret of a good press release?

Any press release is the result of hard work and attention to detail. The structure and layout of a release is fairly rigid, so the creative spark that catches a journalist's attention comes from the text itself.

The first thing to get right is the layout, which should leave journalists space for notes and editing marks. Good practice is to:

- Use A4 paper (or size if emailed) with 1 to 1.5 inch (2.54 to 3.17cm) margins all round;

- Include your organisation's name, address, and your contact details prominently at the top of the page (left, centre or right makes little difference);

- Beneath it include the release date and time. If an embargo is being used, indicate the date and time;

- A headline should be written in 12 point capitals and underlined, or in underlined normal lettering of 16 to 18 point size;

- Format the text in 12 point double line spacing. The first page must never end mid-paragraph, so include 'More follows' and begin the next paragraph on the second page;

- Write 'Ends' at the end of the release, and never go over two pages in length.

Journalists write news stories using a structure called the inverted pyramid. Press releases should follow this format. The two opening paragraphs tell the whole story in about 40-60 words, and contain the answers to the questions: Who, What, Why, Where, When and How. The remaining three to five paragraphs add extra information, usually a quote from a spokesperson and background on your organisation.

You must write as skilfully as journalists to make your releases effective. This means treading a fine line between your organisation's publicity needs and the media's news requirements.

> **HINT**
>
> Compare a range of newspaper articles and press releases to see how they use the inverted pyramid. Sample releases can be found at **www.irishpressreleases.ie, www.press.ie** and **www.prnewswire.co.uk**. Be warned! Some are better written than others.

See also

Q53   What do I put into a press kit?

Q55   What should I avoid when writing a press release?

Q56   What content goes in a holding statement?

Q55   What should I avoid when writing a press release?

Since the purpose of a press release is to convey information in a clear and interesting way, anything that prevents it being used by the media is to be avoided.

There are several sins that must be avoided:

- Overly clever headlines with puns;
- Bad grammar, spelling, punctuation and random capitalisation of words. Word processing packages include a spelling and grammar check, so there is no excuse for distributing a release littered with errors;
- Acronyms and abbreviations, unless very well known;
- Jargon and industry-specific language unless you are writing for the trade press;
- Clichés, catchphrases and fad words. '*Going forward*, the *bottom line* is that these words, though adding a *unique dimension* to one's writing, have passed their *sell-by date*' illustrates the point;
- Unnecessary foreign words, adjectives and adverbs included simply for effect;
- Slang.

Releases should be written in a journalistic style, so avoid writing 'puff' – material that reads like an advertisement, or is written to please management or a client.

Sending one generic press release to a variety of media outlets also is to be avoided. Tailoring a press release so that it is specific for each outlet, though time-consuming, is preferable – and gets better results.

HINT

The Plain English Campaign is a UK-based organisation that promotes simple communication, especially in press releases and official documents. It has free guides on writing style, and software that can highlight bad writing in press releases posted online. See **www.plainenglish.co.uk**.

See also

Q53   What do I put into a press kit?
Q54   What's the secret of a good press release?
Q56   What content goes in a holding statement?

Q56   What content goes in a holding statement?

A holding statement is a short press release usually issued when a crisis has just struck. The need to begin communicating immediately with the media must be balanced with the need to include accurate information. The holding statement is a compromise between these needs: it provides basic information quickly, with a promise of more as soon as new information is known.

While a press release may be up to two pages long, a holding statement rarely exceeds one. It will have the same layout as a standard press release.

You should begin by expressing regret that an incident has occurred, and concern for victims, their families, and other affected parties.

Next, give basic information on what has happened. Your statement must stick to what is known, even if the information is scant. Contradictory information should be set aside until it can be clarified for inclusion in a later release. You should never speculate about the causes of the crisis, suggest likely outcomes or attribute responsibility.

The statement should state that your organisation is doing everything possible to address the situation, and give journalists a realistic timeline for updated information so they can work around their editorial deadlines.

A draft holding statement can be written in advance and included in your organisation's crisis manual, ready for use with just a little tweaking required. Bear in mind that, such is the speed of social media and online citizen journalism, journalists can arrive at the scene of a crisis armed with more information than you have been able to include in your statement, so time taken to quickly scan online coverage may be well spent.

See also
Q54   What's the secret of a good press release?
Q55   What should I avoid when writing a press release?

Q57   Can I write a feature article and use it for publicity purposes?

A feature article is a great way of focussing on a particular aspect of your organisation, or advocating a point of view. It is considered soft news and is different to a press release:

- It is written exclusively for one publication;
- It is longer (around 750 to 1,000 words) and tends to last longer than news;
- It uses a beginning, middle and end structure, not the inverted pyramid;
- An idea for a feature should be pitched to an editor, not submitted speculatively;
- Newspapers may request features from prominent organisations to highlight an issue of public importance;
- Greater depth and detail on an organisation, its people and activities can be given;
- A feature can be written as part of a series, appearing at regular intervals.

Features appeal to a wide readership, and have something interesting to say. Broadly speaking, there are a few main categories:

Type of feature	Example
The **profile feature** focuses on an individual, presenting them as a whole person, rather than in the narrow confines of their job. Aspects of the person's private life, background, hobbies or sporting achievements can allow readers to better understand the person's role. Similar to this is the **organisational feature** which, by profiling employees, brings the reader behind the scenes of your organisation.	A profile of the director of nursing in a hospital can use their life story to illustrate their job. Was there a special event that led them to become a nurse? How have memories of their first day on a ward influenced their role as a manager of hundreds of nurses? A day in the life of student nurses on a busy ward can offer insights into the hospital itself.
The **human interest feature** takes an 'against all odds' focus. It is commonly used by health charities that have a patient advocate who is willing to share their story.	A transplant patient who wins a medal at the World Transplant Games can draw attention to the charity they represent.
The **product or service feature** must be done subtly or it will read like an advertising piece. These features are built around somebody whose life or work has changed by using the product or service. This is especially suited to healthcare and lifestyle products and services.	A feature about a successful agribusiness could explain how the farmer uses apps on his smart phone to record data about livestock or crops. The brand of phone would be named 'incidentally' to the main part of the story.
The **advocacy feature** allows an organisation to put forward its ideas for addressing a problem, or starting a debate about an issue.	A representative body for small business could start a public debate about the need for state investment in ecommerce infrastructure.

See also

Q61 What is an advertorial?

Q58   What makes a good publicity photograph?

It is easier to say what makes a bad publicity photograph. There are several types that stand out for sheer awfulness and lack of imagination:

- The politician or businessperson at their desk, phone to their ear, tapping at a keyboard, or intently studying a document;

- A line of people, with a corporate logo in the background. The banality of this shot is made worse if they are pretending to read copies of a report, held at an unnatural angle so the viewer can see the cover;

- A sporting trophy or outsized cheque being presented over a handshake.

For best results, establish what kind of photograph is needed: a head and shoulders shot of the CEO for the website or annual report, photographs of products for glossy magazines, or a photo opportunity for the national press require different techniques.

In consultation with the photographer, plan the shoot and the intended response the photographs will have.

The type of photograph currently popular in newspapers tends to emphasise:

- **Context:** A photograph of the person doing their job, especially if it involves complex equipment or safety clothing, adds to the story the picture is telling;

- **Natural pose:** This is important for photographs accompanying a human interest story, and is also very effective for business or political photography;

- **Proper lighting:** Over- or under-lit photographs will not reproduce well in print unless they are edited using software, which is time-consuming and reduces the quality of the image;

- **Photographs on location:** These can create a mental association for the viewer of the person or organisation. Think of the image created by a photograph of an award-winning baker standing in a field of ripening wheat;

- Good composition: Most group photos have no more than three people in shot. Intrusive corporate logos are not in view;
- The right people in shot: Only those who are directly relevant to the story should appear in a shot for the press. This can be relaxed slightly if models or children are being used;
- A visually creative composition that stands out over other photographs.

HINT

Nothing beats forethought for photography. When planning photographs for the press, go through every newspaper a week or two beforehand to see what kind of images they prefer.

See also
Q44   How do I organise a photo call?
Q46   How do I brief a photographer?
Q59   When should I write an extended picture caption for a photograph?

Q59   When should I write an extended picture caption for a photograph?

Most photographs are sent as an accompaniment to a press release, so captions are short, usually no more than 20 words. They identify who is in the photograph and why it was taken, and refer the journalist or photo editor to the press release for the whole story. Their purpose is to add a visual context to the story and draw the reader in.

Sometimes, it may be preferable to send a photograph on its own. A photograph can record or publicise an event of minor significance that has already been, or will be, covered in more detail as part of a bigger story. In such cases, an extended caption of 40 to 60 words can convey the who, what, why, where, when and how needed to tell the story:

- The town bank manager presenting a cheque to the local branch of a charity hardly merits a full press release to the local newspaper, especially if the presentation is the follow-up to a story about the launch of an appeal reported on some weeks previously. An extended caption can remind readers about the launch of the appeal, the bank's involvement and the good work the charity does;

- A hotel promoting a wedding fair will find that wedding magazines are full of rivals promoting such events. A photograph of models posing as a bride and groom in an unusual setting can act as a quirky visual element to the story, which gives the location, date and names of some key exhibitors at the fair in the extended caption;

- The appointment of a new manager will receive, at best, a two or three line snippet in the news digest section of a newspaper. A photograph of the person in an activity connected to their job, with an extended caption detailing their name, new job, previous experience and ambitions for the role may receive better coverage.

Extended captions are less widely used than the press release and photograph combined, but can be very effective in their own right.

See also
Q44 How do I organise a photo call?
Q46 How do I brief a photographer?
Q58 What makes a good publicity photograph?

Q60   What content should go in a newsletter or e-zine?

Content depends on the kind of newsletter an organisation produces. Newsletters for external publics need professional writing with high quality illustrations. Those for staff may be less formal. Every type of publication needs editorial guidelines on content and presentation style.

Type of newsletter	Purpose	Suggested content
In-house	Inform, train and entertain staff. Foster loyalty. Create a sense of belonging.	News about your organisation. News about your industry/sector. Training features. Employee profiles. Achievements of individual staff. Social news.
Consumer	Raise consumer awareness of products and services. Initiate trial and purchase. Build reputation, trust and brand loyalty.	Tips on saving money or time using your organisation's product. Sponsorships, CSR activities, etc. Recent awards. Testimonials.

Type of newsletter	Purpose	Suggested content
Trade and business to business	Raise awareness with suppliers and business customers. Initiate trial and purchase. Provide technical information on product use/operation.	Articles on products (new designs, specifications, uses). Profile a client using your product. Reports from trade shows. New staff appointments. Awards and industry quality marks. Client/customer testimonials.
NGO and charity	Advocacy. Fundraising. Public awareness. Link national and local branches. Build community. Share experiences.	Profiles of staff, members, volunteers, and clients. Reports on fundraising events, conferences, AGMs. Reports on lobbies and campaigns. Motivational articles. Open letters to politicians.

The content must be something readers want to read, but delivering this takes editorial skill and effort. Reminding management that content communicates, not bores, is often a full-time job. Newsletters and e-zines succeed when they have a variety of articles of about 50 to 500 words. The best ones include some form of response mechanism – a way of enticing the reader into communicating with the organisation, for example:

- **Consumer:** Customer queries and replies, competitions, redeemable vouchers;
- **Trade:** 'Ask the expert' column;
- **NGO and charity:** Survey of how readers are affected by an issue.

See also
Q11   What are the main tools of internal communications?

Q61   What is an advertorial?

Advertorial is a mixture of 'advertisement' and 'editorial'. It is a piece of writing, usually in the form of a feature article with accompanying photographs, whose inclusion in a newspaper or magazine has been paid for by your organisation.

Advertorial is usually written by a journalist of the publication, under their by-line, or anonymously by you or a freelance journalist in behalf of your organisation. It will be similar in layout to the rest of the publication, using similar typeface, line spacing and font size. To make it distinct, it contains an acknowledgement that is a paid-for feature. Usually, a phrase like 'Commercial Feature', 'Advertising Feature' or something similar will appear at the top of the article.

Advertorials are popular as they guarantee your organisation that its message will appear in the media. They are considered useful for consumer products or services that are very low in news value and would struggle to get press coverage. Because they are similar in appearance to regular news items, it is believed they are more credible than advertisements.

However, their obvious similarity to regular editorial may be seen as an attempt to deceive readers. Misuse of advertorials may lead to complaints being investigated for breaches of the codes of practice of the Advertising Standard Authority of Ireland, or, in the UK, the Code of Advertising Practice.

See also
Q57   Can I write a feature article and use it for publicity purposes?

Q62 How do I write a speech?

Making a speech can be scary and even experienced speakers can feel nervous. It need not be that way. Preparation is everything. Usually, speeches are the result of an invitation to address a gathering, a business pitch, or an address to employees – but they all start with the same considerations:

- Who is the audience?
- Why are they there?
- What are their expectations?

If the theme of the speech has been left to you to decide, this is the next stage to address:

- How can the theme be expressed? Should it be persuasive (a business pitch), entertaining (an after-dinner speech at a charity function), or informative (addressing staff)?
- What case studies, facts, anecdotes, stories and so on bring the theme to life?
- What message should your audience take away with them?
- Research information for the main points that will help the theme to develop.

Ordering points helps a structure to emerge. There are many ways of structuring a speech, though all should tell a story. Some popular structures are:

- **Say what will be said, say it, and say what was said**: This is the simplest speech, and is one that is helpful for nervous speakers;
- **The beginning, middle and end**: After an attention-grabbing opening, the speech can use a chronological (time-line), topical (one subject at a time) or causal (how one issue affects another) approach;
- **The call to action:** This outlines a problem, suggests ways to resolve it and seeks commitment to act.

Now, the writing can begin! Here are a few good writing tips you should remember:

- Though written, a speech is intended to be heard, not read;
- Keep the language simple, with short sentences that sound like normal speech;
- Keep an eye on grammar, jargon and idioms that may prevent your message being heard;
- Give the introduction, each point and the conclusions their own paragraphs for clarity. Link each paragraph to the next one;
- Using 'we' creates a bond with your audience;
- Allow a rate of about 150 words per minute to guide the length.

| HINT | To sharpen up a speech, delete every adjective and adverb in the draft. If the speech makes its point without them, it did not need them in the first place. |

See also
Q63   How do I write a speech for somebody else to deliver?

Q63 How do I write a speech for somebody else to deliver?

Writing a speech for a client or manager uses the same process as writing for oneself. The audience and theme are identified, the points conveying the central message decided on, and the speech gets written. The difference is that the person delivering it did not write it, and the success of the speech depends on how well you and the speaker work together.

Before meeting the speaker, get information to fill in a checklist. This includes information about the audience, venue, occasion, details of other speakers, theme, duration and available audiovisual equipment. This can be done by email or telephone, and saves a lot of time.

At the first meeting, you need to:

- Understand how the speaker thinks, feels and sounds by asking broad questions about their likes, dislikes, life experiences and so on. These will highlight the client's values, strengths, weaknesses, interests, and good and bad biases;

- Ask why you are needed: is the speaker too busy, or not confident about public speaking? A speaker who is not confident will need a speech tailored to their personality and abilities;

- Agree a schedule for writing, revising and approving the speech;

- Discuss the theme and key points. Ask for any stories, anecdotes or facts the speaker wants to use to illustrate these;

- Make notes, or record the speaker discussing these points. Their words can be tidied up for inclusion in the speech, ensuring that it matches the way they speak. The goal is to achieve a polished speech with a ring of authenticity.

The first draft should be sent to the speaker, who can highlight any points, words or phrases they are uncomfortable with. This helps you to fine-tune new drafts, until the speaker approves the speech.

To finish, you should format the speech for an A4 page with generous margins, 16 point font, double line spacing, and page numbers, before giving the client hard and electronic copy.

See also
Q62   How do I write a speech?

Q64   How do I prepare for a broadcast interview?

Television, radio and webcast interviews are excellent ways to communicate. They have potentially very large audiences, and the programme, presenter or journalist can add credibility to the interview.

Walking into a studio for the first time can be unsettling as the soundproofing alters the atmosphere. Even an interview in a familiar place can be daunting. Fortunately, the preparation you do can help you to overcome nerves and concentrate on your message.

Stage of preparation	What to do
Background preparation	Research the media outlet, and the journalist asking the questions. Is the interview live or recorded? Who are the audience? Will their queries be put to you? Anticipate and prepare answers to questions that focus on three key messages.
The message	Focus on sound-bites, not statements. A quote for a news bulletin rarely exceeds seven seconds. Make issues generic, not particular to avoid undesirable debate.

Stage of preparation	What to do
Physical appearance	Wear smart, comfortable, co-ordinated clothing without checks, stripes, bright reds and white as these cause problems for TV cameras. A conservative look (dark, but not black, suit and tie or scarf) usually works. Shirts and blouses look best in pastels. Jewellery should be subtle and not distracting, even on radio, as microphones will pick up jangling bracelets. Beards and moustaches should be trimmed. Hair should be trimmed, or, if long, pulled back, especially if the interview takes place outside. Accept studio make-up: it eliminates sheen from the skin, and covers 'five o'clock shadow' on men. For interviews in the organisation's headquarters, choose a place that is well-lit, quiet and tidy. A TV crew may want some background footage, while a radio producer may want ambient noise.
Voice, gestures and where to look	Your tone of voice should be normal and natural, and support the message. Experienced interviewees often use a slightly lower register to sound more authoritative, but this takes practice. Gestures should be polite and controlled. A rule of thumb is to ensure your elbow is at most a hand-span from your ribs when gesturing, even on radio as gestures can pull you away from the microphone. Always look at the interviewer or other guest, if responding to them. Never look directly at the camera.

Remember that it is good to practice, but not at the expense of freshness and spontaneity.

In Practice

Avril Mulcahy owns one of Ireland's most successful dating and matchmaking agencies, Singlelista. She is constantly in demand as a media commentator on relationships, and has amassed a string of national television and radio appearances. Good preparation has been a contributing factor to her media success. Among her tips for a successful interview is concentrating on finding the right presenter to pitch an idea to, rather than focussing on a potential audience. A knowledgeable interviewer can identify elements in any story to which their audience can relate. She also stresses the importance of being introduced with a specific title, and of endeavouring to make the presenter look and sound good through meticulous planning and attention to detail. Sensibly, she advises calling the presenter or their production team after the interview to ask how they felt it went.

See also

Q41   When could I use narrowcasting instead of broadcasting?

ENGAGING ONLINE

Q65 What social media sites can I use for PR?

Social media has broader meaning than socialising or networking online. Many organisations focus heavily on blogs, microblogs and social networks, and not enough on other applications.

Social media type	Examples	How they work
Blogs	Use blog-specific search engines like **technorati** or **searchengineland** for examples.	Writers give their views on topics, and can invite feedback. Organisations can write their own blogs, or communicate with bloggers as they would journalists.
Bookmarking Sites	Delicious. Pinterest. Stumbleupon.	These allow users to save and manage links to various websites for easy access. These links can then be shared with other users.
Forums and chat rooms	Boards.ie. Digital Spy.	Forums allow members to have conversations in 'threads' – a sequence of posted comments on a topic. Some forums focus on a specific interest, while others encompass many interests.

Social media type	Examples	How they work
Media Sharing	Flickr. Vimeo. YouTube.	These sites allow users to upload and share videos, photographs, podcasts and so on. Because they allow comments from viewers, they allow users to converse with each other. It is possible to restrict access, so that only those users you want to share material with can access it.
Microblogging	Tumblr. Twitter.	These are sites where users create very short messages to all users, or defined groups. They work in real time, so your followers can receive instant updates, conversations and promotional offers.
Social Networks	Bebo. Facebook. LinkedIn. Yammer.	Users connect with people and organisations with whom they have something in common. Users create a unique profile that communicates their identity and interests. Users choose how they want to interact with other users through 'liking' things they post, endorsing them, creating closed groups and so on.

Social media type	Examples	How they work
Social News	Digg. Newsvine. Reddit.	These sites provide news to users, either directly on the sites, or by links to other sites. Users vote on items – the more votes an item gets, the more prominently it is displayed. Community moderation makes it hard to manipulate content.
Wikis	WikiHow. Wikipedia.	A wiki is a website that allows collaborative creation of content (the name is an acronym of 'what I know is'). Users can create, edit or delete material, even if it has been created by others.

There can be an overlap of functions on social media sites, and not all fit into one category. Facebook facilitates microblogging, for example, while many forums also have members' blogs.

See also
Q66   How do I use social media for building relationships?
Q67   How do I publicise my presence on social media?
Q68   How do I use social media for promotions?

Q66 How do I use social media for building relationships?

Too often, organisations measure their success on social media by their number of friends or followers. In real life, nobody counts friends and family members: they work hard at maintaining relationships with them.

In social media, numbers are not the target. Good relationships are. If your organisation sells only in Cork or Manchester, it is better to have a relationship with 500 followers nearby than 10,000 abroad.

There are some simple pointers to building relationships online:

- **Be authentic**: Be genuine in your interaction with publics. Accept that when you invite comments some will be negative, and address them. Never write fake blogs (flogs) or create false identities to write great reviews or run down rivals: you will be found out, and will get the attention those actions deserve;

- **Listen:** Pause and listen to what your followers are saying, about you, their needs, life in general, or whatever. You will learn more about their concerns and preoccupations. Understanding leads to better communication;

- **Build trust**: When your communication is interesting, distinctive and tailored to their needs, your followers trust you more and become your advocates. By retweeting, pinning, liking and more, they tell their followers that they trust you;

- **Reward followers**: When followers recommend you to their own followers, thank them. Reward them with special offers when they write good reviews or positive articles on their blogs. Even praise and recognition are good rewards if they cannot physically avail of your offers;

- **Manage resources**: If your social media presence extends over many sites and includes blogging or podcasting, make sure you have the resources to maintain your activity. Irregular updates, occasional tweets, or delays in responding to comments may be more damaging than having a lower, but manageable, presence;

- **Network**: When you meet people connect with them online afterwards.

HINT

Politicians often find that followers do not yield votes. When party members, media, rivals and lobby groups, for example, are discounted perhaps only a small percentage of followers live in their constituency, and fewer again vote for them. Analyse your followers to see who your 'constituents' are – the publics on whom you depend, and pay them special attention.

See also

Q65   What social media sites can I use for PR?
Q67   How do I publicise my presence on social media?
Q68   How do I use social media for promotions?

Q67 How do I publicise my presence on social media?

No matter how good your social media presence, you have to promote it.

The first stage is to make sure that the people you know are aware that you have a social media presence, so tell them. An email announcing that you have a Twitter account may create little excitement, but a special offer for the first 100 people to retweet something from your account may create more interest.

Search for your customers and associates on social networks like LinkedIn or Facebook. This can be done by letting the network search your emails for addresses that match their users. Once connected, every time you update your profile, they will receive a notification, making it easy for them to follow you.

Link to as many organisations and people as possible. Instead of asking customers to 'like' you on Facebook, like them first.

Use QR codes. There are several websites that allow you to generate these codes that can be scanned by a smart phone. Include your Twitter, Facebook or other social media address in the code to bring people straight to the site.

Corporate social responsibility (CSR) programmes can be useful too. Reward retweets, likes and pins by making a donation to a charity. Use your presence to publicly support charities and not-for-profit campaigns.

Include your social media addresses as a signature in all your email correspondence.

Finally, don't forget that offline promotion also works:

- Use competitions, special offers and give-aways as incentives to get customers to sign-up as followers;
- Put your social media addresses on vehicle livery, uniforms, stationery, pens, t-shirts, umbrellas and other items;

- Instead of 'your call is important to us' messages in your telephone hold music, invite callers to visit you online.

See also

Q65   What social media sites can I use for PR?
Q66   How do I use social media for building relationships?
Q68   How do I use social media for promotions?
Q75   How does search engine optimisation work?

Q68   How do I use social media for promotions?

The only limit to using social media for promotions is your imagination and creativity. The instant nature of the communication and the wide range of its uses make it ideal for promotions. Be mindful, though, your promotional activity follows the rules of the social network you use.

Consider:

- **Special offers:**
  - Use Twitter and Facebook to announce special time-limited offers only for your followers: The next 100 customers to use a key phrase receive a discount or gift when paying, for instance;
  - Offer coupons: Facebook lets you design coupons that are activated when somebody likes your page;
  - Giveaways: Free samples of products, or small gifts that say something about your organisation can create positive publicity.
- **Competitions:**
  - Best picture: Offer prizes for the best photograph of your product being used in unusual settings, or on a set theme;
  - Best video: Get followers to create 30 second adverts for your product or service;
  - Style icons: If you work in fashion or the beauty industry, pin a celebrity photo to Pinterest each day and get followers to vote for their weekly style icon. Give a prize to a follower who voted for the weekly winner. Replace 'style' with 'sport' and it works for sportswear retailers, publishers, bookmakers and so on;
  - 'Pin to win' competitions on Pinterest: Followers pin photos on a theme. A restaurant, for example, could offer a free meal to followers who pin photos of their ideal dinner party guests, featuring celebrities and historical figures. A football club could offer a season ticket to fans who pin their all-time best players;
  - Raffles: Get followers to follow a link on your site to an entry form for a prize.

These are simple, easy-to-organise techniques. Once you get used to using social media for promotions, you can start to use more advanced techniques like video games on your social network, scavenger hunts and so on.

See also
Q65   What social media sites can I use for PR?
Q66   How do I use social media for building relationships?
Q67   How do I publicise my presence on social media?

Q69   What is a blog?

A blog is an online journal. It comprises short articles presented in chronological order with the latest first, where you present information or opinions to readers. Blog sites are easy to set up, either on dedicated blogging sites, or on sites owned by an organisation.

Blogs are a recent development in online communication. The earliest blogs were text-based, but now images, audio and video files, and links to other websites are common features. This has increased their attractiveness to organisations:

- Blogs can promote transparency by addressing publics directly. Many blogs now have feedback options and encourage readers to enter into a debate with the blogger;

- This open interaction also humanises organisations: the CEO or a team of bloggers can become the personal face of your organisation;

- Some bloggers become well-known as influential thought leaders in society and industry;

- Media relations can be enhanced, as many journalists follow blogs for information.

Blogging does not suit every organisation, however. A blog requires time and effort to keep it fresh and interesting. 'Me-tooing' – blogging because all your rivals or industry partners are doing it – is never a good reason to blog. Organisations and individuals – particularly political parties and politicians – that see blogs as a place to copy and paste bland press releases will drive readers away in boredom.

The best blogs are well-written, thought-provoking, regularly updated and engage in a conversation with readers. The ultimate aim is to build relationships with your publics, and how better than by offering them high quality content?

HINT

To ensure that readers don't see your blog once only, make sure you have a 'Subscribe' button on the blog page. Subscriptions enable readers to receive your blogs by email or RSS feeds, and allow them to post comments on your blog page.

See also
Q70   Is writing a blog hard?

Q70 Is writing a blog hard?

Writing a blog is easy. Anybody can do it, but many blogs are uninspiring. Writing a good blog takes a lot of planning and hard work. The reason why most fail to communicate is that many organisations and writers do not understand why they are blogging, or underestimate the necessary commitment.

The key elements are:

- **Planning:**
  - Start by deciding why your organisation should have a blog. Is it to promote products, enhance its reputation, or to connect with like-minded people and organisations?
  - Who is your intended audience?
  - Who will be responsible for writing material and updating it?
  - What will the blog be about – it should say something that people will want to read. Articles about how great your business is will quickly turn readers off. Instead, think about what your organisation can say about its sector, or issues it faces with its publics;
  - Choose the tone that best communicates with publics. Blogs have an informal style of writing, which makes them very readable, and often address readers directly.

- **Content:**
  - Keep content interesting, relevant and up-to-date;
  - Content can be news about your organisation, an interview with somebody of interest to readers, an opinion piece on an issue, a book review, how-to guides and tips;
  - Blog posts should be short, 200-500 words is an ideal length. Paragraphs should be short, around one or two sentences;
  - Start with a big headline that grabs readers' attention. Follow this with three or four sentences that give the blog a high impact opening, and draw readers in;
  - Use subheadings in a larger font size and images to break up the text;

- Include links to other sites that readers may find interesting;
- Remember that a blog will start a conversation with readers, so provide them with well-thought out material, and allow space for feedback and comments. Always reply to comments that need a response;
- Never post for the sake of it: a blog should always have something to say

- **Frequency:**
  - Set a schedule for posting blogs. Keep to it. Blogs need fresh material, so there should be at least a main post every week, with shorter posts every other day. Share the responsibility around the office if it is too much for one person;
  - Create a store of blog posts on general topics to use when there is not enough time to write a blog.

See also
Q69   What is a blog?

Q71   Why will people want to listen to my podcast?

A podcast is a cross between a radio broadcast and an audio weblog. It has much in common with narrowcasting in that listeners are likely to share what may be a common niche interest. All that is required to get started is basic equipment and software to record and edit good quality material:

- A microphone and headset with either a digital recorder, computer, tablet, or smartphone is fine for simple podcasts, though complex ones need a mixer;
- Some computers have pre-installed editing software, and there are also easy to learn shareware (free) packages;
- Podcasts take up a lot of bandwidth, so your server must be able to handle large amounts of data. Sites like Podcastalley do not store podcasts. They provide 'RSS feeds': little files that, when clicked, bring people to podcasts, which are hosted elsewhere.

The better your equipment and editing skills, the more professional your podcast will sound, which will attract and retain listeners. Technical issues aside, what makes a podcast interesting?

- **Length:** Most podcasts run for 30 to 60 minutes;
- **Frequency:** Make sure the podcast comes out at the same time, all the time. Weekly is ideal, but producing an hour's worth of material takes about a day, so be realistic;
- **Format:** Will the podcast be a monologue, panel discussion, series of interviews, vox-pops, or a mixture? Choose an appropriate format: a charity trying to increase awareness of an issue could use longer human interest pieces and expert interviews, while a fashion retailer aiming at the youth market could use a faster format with many short segments;
- **Content:** This links the message you want to convey with what your publics want to hear. They want to be entertained and

informed, not lectured to! Keep content varied, planned and scripted to ensure it always sounds fresh and relevant.

Of course, great content is wasted if nobody knows about it so:

- Include the RSS feed in all your organisation's emails, social media sites and website;
- Include the RSS feed or the audio file in electronic press kits;
- Instead of hold music on your telephone, play the latest edition of the podcast.

| HINT | Before creating your podcast, go to iTunes, Blubrry and Podcastalley and subscribe to podcasts on your own sector to hear how other podcasts are produced. |

See also
Q20   What are controlled media?
Q41   When could I use narrowcasting instead of broadcasting?

Q72   What is a dark site?

Although the term could be thought of as slightly sinister, a dark site is simply a version of your website created in anticipation of a crisis and hosted on a server but not online.

When a crisis strikes, your website is the first place media and publics turn to for information. How quickly you respond determines whether you will be seen as a credible source, or bypassed. Your regular website can be replaced within minutes by a dark site containing essential information.

There are three options for presenting a dark site:

- Fully removing the existing website and replacing it with the dark site should only be done for crises of the highest gravity;
- Retaining the existing website and linking from it to the dark site hosted under a different domain name;
- Creating a dark site that blends the crisis management element with the website's regular features is suitable for crises that do not interrupt the organisation's activities.

Because traffic to the website is likely to increase substantially, you should assess what level of traffic your Internet server can cope with, and be prepared to create a mirror site if needed. A mirror site is an exact copy of your website hosted on another server.

Usually a dark site includes:

- A holding statement prominent on the homepage;
- Contact e-mail addresses and telephone numbers on the homepage;
- A secure log-in staff section with crisis management protocols, or where management can address staff concerns privately;
- A press room where updates can be posted;
- General information on the organisation, management, products and services.

For a dark site to be truly effective, all your online communication should be channelled through it. That means that social media sites should be cleared of all previous content, and new posts should relate only to the crisis. Links to social media sites should be prominent on the homepage and, where possible, include live feeds from them so the dark site becomes the central hub for all your online crisis communication.

See also
Q95   What goes in my crisis kit?
Q96   How should I respond to a crisis?

Q73   What is an electronic press kit?

An electronic press kit is simply a more modern version of the traditional press kit and is intended for use by the same media publics.

However, because it is not in printed format, the electronic press kit is far more dynamic and versatile. As well as the usual press release, biographies and backgrounders found in traditional press kits, electronic kits can include:

- Audio files such as podcasts, interviews, or comments suitable for radio news bulletins. Entertainment PR practitioners also include music and soundbites from singers and films they are promoting;

- Video files such as short corporate videos, advertisements, music videos and cinema trailers;

- Offline versions of your organisation's website, or website links;

- Low and high resolution photographs. High resolution photographs are ideal for reproduction in newspapers and glossy magazines, while low resolution versions, which load faster on computers, are suitable for quickly looking over, or posting on websites;

- Software and games. For organisations in the technology sector, providing trial or beta versions for reviewing purposes allows journalists to try out what may be an expensive product without compromising their code of ethics on accepting free samples. Trial versions typically allow a limited number of uses before they expire, or do not allow full access to all the product's features.

Electronic press kits offer some advantages for distribution over traditional press kits:

- Journalists can receive electronic press kits as attachments or links in emails;

- They can be saved as PDF files and posted on the organisation's website for anybody to access;

- They can be saved to CDs, DVDs or USB flash drives.

See also

Q37　Why won't a journalist accept my press kit and free samples?

Q53　What do I put into a press kit?

Q74 Should I control which employees can update my social media accounts?

In a word: yes!

It only takes one disgruntled employee to sabotage a carefully executed online campaign. Similarly, it only takes one moment of inattentiveness for an employee to post inappropriate content on your Facebook page rather than their own. Less troubling, but no less serious, a junior manager may not understand your communication strategy.

Online relationships are too valuable to leave in the hands of every employee. Not every employee can be, or expects to be, an official spokesperson.

Identify which employees need to be able to update your social media accounts. This would probably include:

- The PR and marketing and customer services managers, and their designated staff;
- Contractors, especially web designers;
- The CEO;
- The HR manager and designated staff for internal accounts. Some organisations use social media accounts like Yammer, which are private networks for organisations and their employees.

Where social media forms a major part of your PR programme, and reaches across different departments, it is advisable to form a team that will agree on a messaging strategy and timelines.

HINT

It is also a good idea to have a HR policy that reminds employees of their responsibilities to the organisation, even when using their own social media accounts. While they may be off-duty when they access them, the media and your publics never are. Revealing company secrets, making unprofessional remarks, uploading videos and photographs or even linking to other sites can reflect badly on your organisation.

See also

Q9   How do PR and human resource management complement each other?

Q76   Why can porosity be bad for an organisation?

Q75   How does search engine optimisation work?

Search engine optimisation (SEO) is the method used to push websites (and pages within them) to the top of search results in search engines like Google, Bing and Metacrawler. Web designers include key words describing each page when they write the programming code of websites. When somebody does a search using any of these words, your website should appear in the first few results.

The most important thing to get right, then, is choosing the keywords that best describe the page, what you do, and, most importantly, what the publics you want to communicate with will use when searching. Because SEO emphasises content as well, it motivates organisations to keep their websites updated with good material. This, obviously, helps it to communicate better with publics.

The more accurate the search result for the web user, the more trustworthy and reliable your website will appear to be. Most web users do not go beyond the first page of results, or even to the last few results on it, so it is important to achieve as high a ranking as possible.

When properly used, SEO can bring visitors to your website much less expensively than paid-for online promotional techniques like pay-per-click and banner advertising. It can also be invaluable in building your brand awareness.

SEO is not an overnight fix that will drive huge volumes of traffic to your website. It takes time and effort to come up with the words, test them, analyse the results, tweak accordingly – and repeat the process for every page, or after every major change to a page. But it is worth doing.

| HINT | Use a measurement package like Google Analytics to see how often visitors come to your website and how they interact with it when there. The information this provides can help you to manage your SEO efforts more efficiently. |

See also
Q67 How do I publicise my presence on social media?

Q76 Why can porosity be bad for an organisation?

Porosity is accidental transparency online. It happens when information leaks out from your organisation unintentionally or incidentally. There are many examples of porosity:

- E-mails are sent to the wrong recipients;
- Information can be put online too early, spoiling product launches or major announcements;
- Employees make reference to their work on their personal or work social media accounts;
- Private pages on a website or intranet for subscribers or employees are accidentally made available for public access;
- A firewall fails to prevent a virus, Trojan or worm from infecting your organisation's computer network, and data is compromised;
- Hackers gain access to confidential information.

Managed porosity – deliberately leaking selective snippets of information – can be a useful tactic at times. Teasers drum up publicity and attract media attention to product launches or, especially in politics, test public reaction to new ideas. Be careful, though, that the information leaked does not do more damage than good to your organisation or its publics.

Being porous can lead to publics mistrusting organisations, and it takes much effort to win back lost trust. It can also lead to data protection regulators taking action against organisations, which further damages reputations.

But there can be good aspects to being porous. Because porosity can do so much damage to reputation and relationships, internal communications with employees can emphasise their own role in managing your organisation's interaction with publics. This can include advising them on how to ensure their own social media use does not include material that could embarrass or damage your organisation.

It also can lead to greater transparency. Leaks that embarrass an organisation can be turned into an advantage if the organisation accepts responsibility, engages with affected publics and reforms its future practices.

See also
Q74   Should I control which staff members can update my social media accounts?

PR EXCELLENCE

Q77   What is a communications audit?

A communications audit measures the effectiveness of your organisation's internal and external communications. Because it analyses how information is given to publics, how they receive it, and how they respond to it, it leads to a better understanding of those publics, and adds to the strategic capabilities of an organisation.

The audit will examine:

What to audit	Considerations
What are your organisation's existing communication skills and resources?	Are they adequate? Are new staff or consultants needed?
What publics are being communicated with, or neglected?	How important are all the publics? Why are some neglected? What can be done to change this?
What are the publics' attitude towards your organisation?	Has your organisation built successful relationships with publics? Do attitudes need to be nurtured or changed?
What information do publics want to receive?	Does it differ from the information being sent out? How?
How effective are channels used to reach publics?	Can the delivery of messages be accurately measured? Do the channels create a dialogue with publics, or is communication one-way? Should different channels be used?
What is the frequency and quality of communication?	Is the volume of communication making it difficult to hear key messages? What is the right balance between enough and too much information?

What to audit	Considerations
What are the barriers to effective communications?	Are they technological, cultural, financial, etc?
Is the communications process cost-effective?	Is the PR function over- or under-staffed? Are new technology, social media, work meetings, etc being used efficiently?

See also

Q78   How do I carry out a communications audit?

Q78   How do I carry out a communications audit?

Communications audits are undertakings that can take several months of planning and research to gather and analyse information. As a rule of thumb, an audit should be carried out about every five years.

The audit may be carried out by employees. They are familiar with your organisation, its policies, procedures, and publics. However, they may be too embedded to have the independence an auditor needs. Your organisation may also find it difficult to justify taking them away from their regular duties for an extended period.

External consultants bring credibility, experience and independence. Because they are seen to offer confidentiality, staff may be more honest with them than with peers conducting the audit.

A communications audit goes through four stages:

Stage	Tasks
Planning	Identify your organisation's communications philosophy – does it have a mission statement, corporate vision, or policies for dealing with publics? Establish how your organisation's short-, medium- and long-term objectives are intended to be communicated. Identify publics and potential publics with whom your organisation may communicate. Identify key areas to examine. Draft and test methods such as questionnaires, one-to-one or small group interviews and focus groups for gathering information from internal and external publics.

Stage	Tasks
Auditing	The audit has three key aspects • **Documentation, symbols and livery** – examine reports, policy documents, memoranda, emails, letterheads, business cards, corporate logos, uniforms, decor, etc to see whether they effectively communicate your organisation's philosophy and objectives; • **Internal publics** – gather views from all or a sample of employees, contractors and agency staff at all levels of the organisation; • **External publics** – gather views from a sample of all publics.
Analysing	Interpret the data and search for common themes from all publics. Test the findings from the documentation, symbols and livery and views of all publics against each other and your organisation's communications philosophy.
Reporting and Recommending	Produce a document for presentation to senior management that will be a framework for communications for the next five-year period. Keep recommendations realistic and achievable.

See also

Q77   What is a communications audit?

Q79   How do I establish my organisation's corporate identity?

Corporate identity is formed by the characteristics that make your organisation different to others. Each organisation has its own personality from which its identity evolves. Corporate identity is a combination of ways that that personality is articulated. Unlike corporate image, which mean different things to different observers, the identity is the same for everybody.

Identity forms over time, often with little strategic thought given by an organisation to how it is characterised. However, it may also be an integral part of strategic communications.

A successful corporate identity can be created by:

- **Logos and symbols:** A corporate logo instantly identifies organisations. Colour schemes also speak volumes: the primary colours in Google's and eBay's logos suggest playfulness and hard work. Proprietary marks like trademarks also contribute, as does packaging;

- **Typefaces:** A serif font, with decorative flourishes on the ends of letters, looks old-fashioned and suits organisations that emphasise tradition or stability. A sans serif font, the type used in this book, has a modern feel. Overly decorative, hard to read fonts should be avoided;

- **Uniforms and livery:** Uniforms can be formal and supplied by the organisation, or an agreed style of clothing that matches the corporate colour scheme. Airlines invest heavily in staff uniforms as it presents a professional and reassuring image. Fast food restaurants use uniforms to create a team environment. The livery of an organisation's transport fleet can suggest reliability and consistency;

- **Behaviour, culture and heritage:** How an organisation conducts itself when dealing with publics says much about its identity;

- **Association with charities and sponsorships:** Organisations show they are good corporate citizens by adopting a charity for a period of time, or engaging in corporate social responsibility (CSR) programmes that benefit their employees and communities.

See also

Q6   What is relationship management?
Q7   What is reputation management?
Q8   How do I manage reputation?
Q80   How do I protect my organisation's corporate identity?

Q80   How do I protect my organisation's corporate identity?

Consistency is one of the most effective ways of protecting corporate identity. Every aspect of your organisation's activities that has communication value, from uniforms and livery, to office decor and culture, should reflect the identity. Five-yearly communications audits should review the corporate identity to ensure that it is being effectively communicated.

Employees are the best people to protect corporate identity. Staff who take pride in working for your organisation will become its best ambassadors. A good induction programme for new staff will lay the foundations for an understanding of their role in protecting the corporate identity.

Attention to detail is important, from ensuring that the website, stationery and office signage all use the exact same shade of colours to thoroughly investigating the pros and cons of undertaking a corporate social responsibility (CSR) programme.

Being proactive is sensible. To protect themselves against criminal gangs' 'phishing' emails, which use legitimate logos and look official, financial institutions have devised customer policies that clearly state they do not engage in email communication that seeks confidential information.

In Practice	Registering trademarks and brands where possible protects against copycat usage. Even unregistered continued usage can help: Victoria Beckham, aka Posh Spice, attempted to prevent Peterborough United football club, known to its fans as 'The Posh', from registering its nickname with the UK Patents Office claiming it infringed her trademark. In response, Peterborough United pointed out that the club's nickname had been in continuous use for 70 years, and its right to be identified by it predated the former Spice Girl's.

See also

Q6   What is relationship management?

Q7   What is reputation management?

Q8 How do I manage reputation?
Q79 How do I establish my organisation's corporate identity?

Q81   What is corporate social responsibility?

Corporate social responsibility (CSR) emerged in business management, and has been adopted by PR practitioners as a way of building relationships with publics that benefit society as a whole.

CSR involves acting with enlightened self-interest – that is, recognising that when your organisation acts responsibly towards society, it also benefits. One of the main principles of CSR is the 'triple bottom line', where your organisation's social and environmental performance is as important as its financial results. This is sometimes called the Three Ps: people, planet and profit.

There are three levels of CSR activity for an organisation:

Level of activity	What it entails
Basic	Your organisation: • Follows the rules of the society in which it operates; • Pays its taxes and dues; • Acts lawfully; • Deals fairly and ethically with staff, customers, clients, associates and other publics.
Organisational	Your organisation: • Follows the spirit of the law – it does not use the law as a shield to permit actions that might be unethical; • Minimises the negative effects its actions can have on publics and the physical environment.
Societal	Your organisation: • Accepts its role in creating a healthy and prosperous society; • Contributes to creating a sustainable physical environment; • Helps to address problems in society; • Thinks globally but acts locally.

Properly managed, CSR can help your organisation to achieve the trust and respect of publics, and to put something back into society. It also can:

- Use environmentally sound practices to reduce costs;
- Reduce risk by identifying and addressing issues;
- Help to recruit the high quality staff needed to be innovative.

CSR should not be used to hide unethical behaviour. There are many examples of clothing brands and retailers that engaged in CSR activities while the garments they sold were made by children in third world sweatshops. CSR is not something that can be bolted on to the way your organisation does business – it must be an integral part of it.

See also
Q82 What kind of activities can be used in corporate social responsibility?
Q83 What is greenwashing?

Q82   What kind of activities can be used in corporate social responsibility?

As long as an activity allows your organisation to show that it takes its social responsibilities seriously – and is not done purely to gain publicity – then it can be regarded as a good activity. It should benefit your organisation, your publics and society at large.

Because CSR is unique to each organisation, it is impossible to list more than a few popular activities. Some of the best CSR programmes are very creative, not just in identifying issues, but in how they use the financial and human resources available to organisations.

Type of activity	Suggested activities
Financial contributions	Sponsorship of charities and worthy causes. Philanthropy – provided that money is given with no expectation of publicity or manipulating opinion. Patronage of organisations, charities and the arts. Donation from purchases of products to a designated charity or campaign.
Gifts and benefit in kind	Providing the organisation's products or services freely. Providing the use of the organisation's buildings, grounds and equipment. Donating obsolete equipment, like computers and mobile phones, to organisations that recycle or recondition them.
Education	Educational and mentoring programmes for the long-term unemployed, school students or marginalised groups. Paid internships for unemployed or marginalised groups. Funding scholarships.

Type of activity	Suggested activities
Environmental practices	Reducing the carbon footprint by initiating recycling, energy awareness, and cycle to work schemes. Stocking work canteens and restaurants with Fairtrade, organic or locally-sourced food produce. Participation in community clean-up days. Sourcing raw materials and other supplies locally where possible.
Ethical employee practices	Offering flexitime, parental leave, and work from home schemes. Avoiding the use of cheap labour, especially sweatshops and unpaid internships that offer no prospect of employment.

See also

Q81   What is corporate social responsibility?

Q83   What is greenwashing?

Q83   What is greenwashing?

Greenwashing is a cynical attempt to benefit from consumers' interest in environmentally sound products and services by making false claims about an organisation's environmental credentials. It is often wrongly regarded as a PR practice, though it has more in common with spin or aggressive marketing techniques, and is ethically wrong.

Even when genuine about their commitment to the environment, organisations should carefully assess the content of their messages in case they inadvertently overstate their case. Some mislead consumers by changing the name of a product or ingredient to make it sound more natural.

Another example is hotels that encourage guests to reuse towels rather than have them replaced daily. While this cuts down on laundering, which consumes a lot of energy, unless the hotel recycles or uses energy efficient lighting, guests may believe hotels abuse their good behaviour to increase the profitability of rooms.

Organisations involved in greenwashing typically spend more money and time promoting their green credentials than they do on being environmentally sound.

Greenwashing may lead organisations to finding themselves on the receiving end of a consumer backlash when their claims are held up to scrutiny. They may also find themselves the subject of scrutiny by regulators, or activist campaigns by environmentalists. The risk of negative attention, when it could be avoided through responsible practice, is another good reason to avoid greenwashing.

See also
Q81   What is corporate social responsibility?
Q82   What kind of activities can be used in corporate social responsibility?

Q84   What is astroturfing?

Astroturfing is a highly dubious tactic employed by some organisations, usually in public affairs or lobbying, but also in consumer affairs. Essentially, astroturfing is when an organisation artificially creates the appearance of widespread public support for a policy, product, organisation or individual.

It is a play on words: it calls to mind, firstly, grassroots campaigns. These are legitimate campaigns where citizens seek to have an issue addressed. Secondly, it alludes to AstroTurf, a synthetic grass surface for sports. Combined, it suggests that some campaigns may be manipulated to give the impression of being legitimate grassroots campaigns.

With the advent of social media and very sophisticated software, it is possible to create multiple online profiles for employees of organisations that are difficult to trace back to their source (this is called sockpuppeting). These profiles are used to support organisations and attack opposition through negative commentary.

It is very difficult to spot astroturfing, and consequently even more difficult to defend an organisation against it. Good relationship management and communication with key publics provide some level of protection against fake campaigns.

PR practitioners who are members of national associations like the Public Relations Institute of Ireland or the Chartered Institute of Public Relations (UK) are obliged to adhere to codes of conduct that prohibit astroturfing.

See also
Q18   What is a pseudo-event?

Q85   What is lobbying?

Lobbying is a specialised PR activity that builds and maintains relations with politicians, especially those in government, in order to:

- Change or retain legislation or regulation;
- Change or retain government policy;
- Negotiate over the awarding of state contracts and licences;
- Persuade opposition politicians to support a campaign.

NGOs and charities also lobby to:

- Build public awareness to put pressure on politicians;
- Access government funding and other supports.

All lobbies seek to demonstrate that an inequality exists, and the organisation is merely seeking fair, not preferential, treatment. They always invoke the public interest as a reason for acting.

Lobbying is sometimes called:

- **Advocacy public relations:** This usually refers to NGOs, charities and less formally organised groups representing interests in society;
- **Public affairs:** This is broader than lobbying, however, and can include communications from governments to the public like referendum information and public awareness campaigns.

Whatever name the practice goes under, lobbying creates relationships with the right people to achieve its goals. While this usually means members of the party of government, its staff and party activists, it also includes:

- Members of the opposition, their staff and party activists;
- Members of local and regional authorities, their staff and party activists;
- The civil and public service, state agencies and other state authorities;

- Members of international organisations such as the EU, United Nations, and their staff.

The typical activities of a lobby include:

- Researching and analysing proposed legislation;
- Monitoring issues to anticipate likely actions;
- Building coalitions with like-minded organisations;
- Educating politicians, their staff and public servants;
- Drafting policy proposals and briefing documents;
- Media relations;
- Event management for public meetings, rallies and marches.

In Practice

The success of a lobbying campaign is not always measured by legislative change: some organisations with long-running issues need to keep their profile high lest interest wanes. To raise awareness of falling farm incomes and the need for political intervention, the Irish Farmers' Association (IFA) mobilised members in a nationwide tractor protest. The 'Tractorcade' of 5,000 farmers and their families passed through 29 towns in a week-long co-ordinated series of demonstrations. The protest culminated outside Government Buildings in Dublin, producing a spectacular image of over 300 tractors lined up in an urban setting that was extensively covered by national media, and even featured on *The New York Times'* front page. For the IFA, the Tractorcade put farming issues back on the political agenda.

See also
Q86 How do I lobby a public authority?

Q86   How do I lobby a public authority?

A lobby starts when your organisation believes a public authority is not treating it equally. A campaign demonstrates the inequality, dramatises it for public support, and brings it to legislators for decision. They may try to block the campaign, so you must anticipate likely responses.

Firstly, legislators may decide to act decisively against it, or to set up a committee to investigate it, hoping the issue will fade before they are forced to act. Secondly, they may argue that:

- The inequality is factually incorrect;
- Your organisation has no right to lobby: granting your demands will create more inequality;
- The effect of legislation on your organisation was unintended;
- They do not have means (financial, time, skills) to resolve the issue;
- It is not in their capacity to make the change; the responsibility rests with somebody else.

With likely counter-arguments identified, your organisation can start to organise its campaign:

Stage	Actions
Preparatory	Define what the issue is, and how it presents an inequality. Identify ideal, acceptable and failed outcomes. Identify key decision-makers – think beyond politicians, and consider special advisers and senior public servants.
Monitoring	Review political activity on new policies or legislation. Lobbies are most effective making a case while laws are being planned. Identify allies and adversaries. Review media coverage of the issue to identify the view of media outlets.

Stage	Actions
Networking	Build coalitions with political allies and like-minded organisations. Open communications with adversaries. Use social media to build popular support.
Raising awareness	Dramatise the lobby to motivate public opinion: use photo calls, public rallies, media campaigns or fundraising opportunities, for instance.
Direct and indirect pressure	Negotiate with politicians, their advisors and senior civil servants. Always have a budgeted, detailed plan showing how the issue can be remedied. Contact other politicians to put pressure on decision-makers. Make the issue an election issue. Avoid activities that create a public nuisance or veer into illegality, like blockades, sit-ins and civil disobedience, as a way of increasing pressure.
Decision	Recognise when a deal is the best available and accept it. Keep the lobby active until the agreement is enacted, not just promised. Never take credit for the result: it undermines politicians, and makes them less likely to deal with your organisation again.

See also
Q85 What is lobbying?

Q87   What is activism?

Activism is the effort by a group of people who share a concern in the social, environmental, economic, or political arena and who campaign for its resolution. Very often, these groups include NGOs, community groups and social movements. They may campaign on a single issue and disappear when it is resolved, or on several issues simultaneously over a long period.

Activism aims to highlight and correct perceived injustices. Activist groups campaign to put pressure on organisations to change, and to legitimise themselves as campaigners for change.

Activism can take many forms. Some of the more typical campaigns include:

Activist areas	Typical campaigns	Who is targeted
Human rights	Freedom of speech. Gender equality. Fair treatment of minorities. Access to justice, medicine and education. Democratic rights.	Governments. International organisations such as the EU, UN, WHO and World Bank. Pharmaceutical companies with patents on medicines. Multinational corporations.
Animal rights	Animal testing in medicine, pharmaceuticals and science. Vivisection. Anti-fur and leather. Vegetarianism and veganism.	Companies and educational institutions involved in animal testing. Fashion designers and shops selling furs.

Activist areas	Typical campaigns	Who is targeted
Environmentalism	Mining, oil and gas exploration, fracking. Global warming. Pollution. Nuclear industry. Alternative energy industry.	Multinational corporations in mining and exploration, energy companies (even those seen as green) air travel, and pharmaceutical industries. Governments and international organisations.
Food	Genetically modified (GM) food. Food additives. Food poverty and world hunger. Cash crops. Sustainable agriculture.	Food industry, including fast food chains, and producers and retailers of GM food. UN, WHO.
Third world issues	International debt forgiveness. Aid and development.	Governments and international organisations.

See also

Q88   What tactics can I use in an activist campaign?

Q89   How do I respond to an activist campaign?

Q88   What tactics can I use in an activist campaign?

Activism works by rallying public opinion around an issue using high profile tactics. Some campaigns are run like lobbies, so the procedure in **Q86** can be followed. Others raise awareness of an issue and put pressure on organisations to change activities or behaviour.

Although some activist groups take a negative view of PR, seeing it as a tactic used against them, this fails to see how relationship management can be used to further their aims.

Direct communication with organisations can be better than megaphone diplomacy. Targeted organisations may wish to negotiate to minimise damage to their relationships and reputation.

Consider the impact your campaign will have on employees of targeted organisations. Lecturing them because their actions are wrong will make them dig in their heels and resist. Outline what the campaign is for, not just against. Activism increases fears about job security and changed work practices, so ensure your campaign minimises these fears.

Building community relations is effective for winning popular support. Activities like family fun days, parades, rallies, town hall meetings, information stands and leaflet drops attract attention.

Many campaigns overlook the importance of media coverage, which can achieve excellent results at little cost – a big factor for small budgets. However, beware of media campaigns conducted by the organisations you target that can negate your efforts.

Internet activism is a growing area that harnesses the power of social media networks. It is an opportunity for activist groups to create communities and share information.

Some popular tactics can fall foul of the law, or anger the publics needed for support. Strikes, civil disobedience, demonstrations, protests, direct action and boycotts do create publicity, and are often favoured by amateur campaigns. But the high risk to reputation and relationships means you should use them only when their consequences have been fully considered.

See also

Q87   What is activism?

Q89   How do I respond to an activist campaign?

Q89   How do I respond to an activist campaign?

Public relations practitioners identify four types of activists, each needing different attention:

Type of activist	How to identify them	How to deal with them
Radicals	They are politically motivated. They mistrust government and the capitalist system. They are dogmatic and inflexible, and offer few concessions. They may be openly hostile.	As their stance influences moderates, they should be dealt with separately. Use the media to reach them. Their inflexibility casts doubt on their credibility and willingness to find a solution, but avoid demonising them.
Idealists	They want a better society, and have a strong sense of justice. They are very credible: because they have no personal gain, their campaigns are seen as altruistic. Publics and media trust them.	Treat them with respect and negotiate. When it makes sense to use their ideas, do so. When their ideas may cause problems, explain the difficulties and negotiate a compromise.
Opportunists	They seek personal gain from campaigns. Fringe political parties often use activism in their electoral strategies.	Victory is important to them, so create a solution where they win some points.

Type of activist	How to identify them	How to deal with them
Realists	They are pragmatic and will negotiate. They will work with the organisation to achieve their goals.	Build strong relationships with them. Co-operate with them. Create joint bodies to address issues.

Your organisation's response dictates how co-operative or obstructive activists will be. Classifying activists as hostile is convenient, but may quickly be labelled as corporate propaganda, and damage the organisation.

There are some general rules for dealing with every activist group:

- **Do not regard activists as the enemy:** Often their campaigns predict future trends, so accepting their views can put your organisation ahead of rivals;

- **Understand how collaboration and compromise work:** Activists dislike them because they seem like a 'sell-out' and organisations dislike the way they disrupt strategic plans. But they are necessary, though they require time and patience;

- **Work hard at bringing activists into the organisation:** This allows dialogue to flourish.

There are some general rules when communicating through the media:

- Become the most reliable source of information on the issue;
- Prevent activists and the media itself from setting the agenda;
- Hold journalists responsible for what they report.

See also
Q87   What is activism?
Q88   What tactics can I use in an activist campaign?

Q90   What is an issue?

An issue is a trend that develops over time with the potential to harm or benefit your organisation. Because issues appear gradually, it is good practice to engage with publics so as to be fully informed of developments in your external environment. Issues can be global, like rising levels of childhood obesity, or rooted in communities, like a plan by a local authority to redevelop a town centre.

Issues are caused by many factors, from political, social and economic, to cultural, moral and ethical. They can be a mixture of two or more of these, or simply how your organisation is perceived. What makes an issue stand out is that it is an unsettled concern waiting to be resolved.

It is tempting to see issues as potential crises, but that is a little simplistic. It is more likely that an ignored issue can cause limited short-term damage that is much less serious than the fall-out from a crisis. Legislation forcing a restaurant to include nutritional information on its menus would be an issue, but, unless the restaurant offered especially unhealthy food and refused to change, it would be unlikely to go out of business.

When an organisation over-emphasises an issue's potential to cause damage, it can lead to a siege mentality that prevents good communication. It is better that issues are seen as potential opportunities for organisations to engage with publics, address problems while they can still be resolved to everybody's satisfaction, and build mutually beneficial relationships.

See also
Q26   How do I carry out a situation analysis?
Q27   What is boundary spanning in PR?
Q91   What is issues management?

Q91   What is issues management?

Issues management is part of your organisation's everyday strategic management. It identifies, analyses and manages issues before they become public knowledge. Key to managing an issue is to know what publics are potentially affected, and how they may respond to it.

There are several ways of analysing the external environment. PR managers have a boundary spanning function: they act as the contact point between an organisation and its external publics. They gather information that alerts them to how the organisation is perceived. This allows them to brief senior managers on how to represent the organisation to these publics.

Another approach is a PESTLE analysis. This examines political, economic, social, technological, legal and environmental factors from which issues may emerge. It offers an overview of where your organisation is at a given point in time.

Issues have their own life cycle. Depending on their stage of development, they can be easy or difficult to manage:

- **Potential:** Use a PESTLE analysis or boundary spanning to identify an issue and its publics;

- **Emerging:** People outside your organisation become aware of it. Up to this point, you can control how the issue develops through proactive communication with publics;

- **Current and emerging:** Other groups, including the media, industry regulators, political agencies, become aware of the issue. There may be increased public pressure to do something about it, and regulatory or political action may follow. This is known as the tipping point. It means that you have lost the ability to directly influence the outcome of the issue;

- **Crisis:** Not all issues reach a crisis point. For those that do, implementing a crisis management campaign becomes critical;

- **Dormant:** An issue that has been addressed to the satisfaction of all stakeholders dies down.

Transparent issues management can produce positive outcomes for an organisation and its publics. However, improperly used, issues management can be seen as an attempt to manipulate public opinion in favour of the organisation. This, of course, should be avoided.

See also
Q26   How do I carry out a situation analysis?
Q27   What is boundary spanning in PR?
Q90   What is an issue?

Q92   What is a crisis?

A crisis is an unexpected event that can have an effect on the reputation, financial stability and trading potential of your organisation, and even lead to closure. It places your organisation under the scrutiny of local, national and international, media, stakeholders and other publics, and regulatory bodies.

An American author, Doug Newsome, lists six types of crisis that cover most situations:

- **Violent acts of nature:** Earthquakes, storms, volcanic eruptions, floods and tsunamis;
- **Non-violent acts of nature:** Droughts and epidemics;
- **Violent intentional human acts:** Criminal and terrorist activity, and product tampering leading to injury, loss of life or destruction of property;
- **Non-violent intentional human acts:** Bomb and product tampering threats, hostile takeovers, illegal corporate activity and malicious rumours;
- **Violent unintentional human acts:** Explosions, fires, chemical leaks, other accidents;
- **Non-violent unintentional human acts:** Product flaws that lead to recalls, stock market crashes and business failures.

By their nature, crises are unpredictable, so no list will cover all possibilities.

Crises become hard news very quickly, and can dominate the news for days or even weeks. Even after a crisis is resolved, organisations need to be alert to anniversaries or similar crises affecting the same industry, as these are events that will rekindle media interest in the organisation.

See also
Q93   What is crisis management?
Q94   How do I prepare to manage a crisis?

Q95   What goes in my crisis kit?

Q96   How should I respond to a crisis?

Q97   Should the most senior manager always be the spokesperson during a crisis?

Q98   What is the difference between an apologia and apology as a response to a crisis?

Q99   How do I use PR to lessen the damage caused by a product recall?

Q100 How do I rebuild my organisation's reputation after a crisis?

Q93   What is crisis management?

Crisis management is the proactive process that makes your organisation assess its internal and external vulnerabilities, and put in place a strategic communications plan for dealing with a range of possible crises. Issues management can prevent some crises from happening, though many will happen without ever having been an issue.

With a crisis management plan, your organisation is less likely to panic and lose control of the communication that is important to maintaining trust and credibility. Although damage will be unavoidable, it may be less than might otherwise have happened if the crisis was badly handled.

Good crisis management starts with expressing regret for what has happened. In the first stages of a crisis, affected publics and society want to hold somebody responsible. A sincere apology will not make the crisis disappear, but it may lessen anger towards your organisation. An offer to cover medical or other costs of affected publics does not admit liability, and can be made at this stage.

This should be followed with an indication of what your organisation will do to ensure that the crisis cannot happen again. A commitment to reform practices, behaviour or manufacturing processes should be made next. It is important that these two steps be a genuine statement of intent, and that reforms are carried out, not just announced and quietly dropped when media interest wanes.

Finally, your organisation should offer restitution or compensation to victims and inconvenienced publics.

See also
Q92   What is a crisis?
Q94   How do I prepare to manage a crisis?
Q95   What goes in my crisis kit?
Q96   How should I respond to a crisis?
Q97   Should the most senior manager always be the spokesperson during a crisis?

Q98   What is the difference between an apologia and apology as a
          response to a crisis?
Q99   How do I use PR to lessen the damage caused by a product recall?
Q100 How do I rebuild my organisation's reputation after a crisis?

Q94   How do I prepare to manage a crisis?

Crises are unexpected events, and no two are the same. Preparing a crisis plan, a template that can be adapted to fit different types of crisis, is excellent management practice.

Crisis planning begins with a risk audit that:

- Identifies the organisation's vulnerabilities and strengths;
- Prioritises the most likely crises;
- Prioritises publics and channels of communication for each one;
- Identifies staff who will form the crisis team, and take responsibility for the crisis kit;
- Identifies training gaps (especially media training).

The audit enables the organisation to arrange training, create an Internet dark site and prepare a crisis manual. This is a short document, about 10 pages, that is kept updated. It guides the crisis team on appropriate messages and tone, and sets out a response timeline.

The manual contains basic information:

- Contact details of every member of the crisis team;
- Contact details of external consultants who may be needed (for instance, PR consultants, technical experts);
- Contact details of journalists likely to cover the story;
- Contact details of regulatory bodies, local authorities and hospitals;
- On- and off-site locations for the crisis team to assemble;
- Lists of human and operational resources that the organisation has, or will need;
- Lists and location of policy documents and industry regulations that need to be followed.

It also will contain some detailed information:

- Background briefs with information on technical matters. These can be prepared for the crisis team's use or for distribution to the media;
- Generic press releases or holding statements with basic fact sheets on the organisation.

The final stage is to run a crisis simulation to test how your organisation and individuals respond. An evaluation of the simulation will identify what issues need to be addressed and will ensure that the team's first attempt at crisis management is not during a real crisis. Even if a simulation exercise is not possible, the crisis team should meet regularly to keep the plan up-to-date.

See also

Q92　What is a crisis?
Q93　What is crisis management?
Q95　What goes in my crisis kit?
Q96　How should I respond to a crisis?
Q97　Should the most senior manager always be the spokesperson during a crisis?
Q98　What is the difference between an apologia and apology as a response to a crisis?
Q99　How do I use PR to lessen the damage caused by a product recall?
Q100　How do I rebuild my organisation's reputation after a crisis?

Q95 What goes in my crisis kit?

Some crises do not affect your organisation's headquarters, so staff can manage the crisis in a familiar environment, with access to everything they need. Fires, natural disasters and major incidents may make the building inaccessible. Telephone lines, work files, employee contact details and computer systems and more are suddenly beyond reach.

To guard against this, your organisation should store a crisis kit off-site, perhaps at the home of a senior manager, where it can be accessed around the clock.

A crisis kit is a small case or holdall containing essential items for managing communications when a crisis breaks. While it will not take the place of a fully operational crisis centre, it will allow your organisation to begin communicating immediately.

A crisis kit contains:

- One or two smartphones and chargers. The phone accounts should be in credit if they are pre-paid numbers. Smartphones offer a range of communications facilities beyond calls and text messages: access to social media sites, e-mails and the organisation's external servers, word processing and document management software, and a camera and video camera. They can also use practical apps – for example, document scanners;

- A laptop and charger configured to access your organisation's intranet, external servers, or online data storage. Your organisation's dark site could be saved on the laptop, which should have up-to-date software and peripherals such as a webcam and portable printer;

- An up-to-date hard and soft copy of the crisis plan, with contact details for the crisis team, senior managers, staff, local authorities, government agencies and hospitals (for crises that require the implementation of a major incident plan), and the media;

- Headed stationery, business cards, notepads, printing paper, pens;

- A petty cash box for incidental purchases.

HINT The crisis kit should be examined periodically to ensure that all the equipment is working and up-to-date.

See also

Q92   What is a crisis?

Q93   What is crisis management?

Q94   How do I prepare to manage a crisis?

Q96   How should I respond to a crisis?

Q97   Should the most senior manager always be the spokesperson during a crisis?

Q98   What is the difference between an apologia and apology as a response to a crisis?

Q99   How do I use PR to lessen the damage caused by a product recall?

Q100 How do I rebuild my organisation's reputation after a crisis?

Q96 How should I respond to a crisis?

There is no better response to a crisis than preparedness. When your organisation has a crisis plan that identifies systems and essential resources, you are better able to respond.

Remove the team from all duties and bring it to a crisis centre with computers, telephones, broadband, printing and copying facilities, and similar facilities for the media. However, to ensure that the team can work in private, there should be no direct access between the centres.

Focus on the immediate implications of the crisis, and assume the worst: if the crisis is worse than the team believes, it may end up drip-feeding the media worsening news, and compromise its credibility. Medium and long-term implications can be considered later.

The team should control all information. Within an hour of the crisis breaking, it should release a holding statement and replace your organisation's website with a dark site. As new information emerges, the dark site should be updated and new statements drafted.

Journalists have tight deadlines and intense competition for stories. While the team may unfairly view them as insensitive and impatient, it should resist combative instincts. Given prompt, accurate information courteously, journalists can help your organisation's response.

Reach out to publics using channels identified in the crisis manual. An apology and facts can calm fears, reduce confusion and reassure publics that your organisation is acting responsibly.

Contain the crisis. If, for example, a food recall is needed only in one region, communications should target local media, and highlight the fact that it has little news value at national level.

Consider a sacrifice. A product recall, or firing the manager responsible for the crisis (not just the employee who caused it), may be unpalatable choices, but they show decisiveness and your intention not to hide anything.

> **HINT**
>
> Your organisation can enhance its media communications during a crisis. Regular briefings by your spokesperson will keep the media informed. Timing briefings to allow journalists meet editorial deadlines will help gain their trust and co-operation.

See also

Q92   What is a crisis?

Q93   What is crisis management?

Q94   How do I prepare to manage a crisis?

Q95   What goes in my crisis kit?

Q97   Should the most senior manager always be the spokesperson during a crisis?

Q98   What is the difference between an apologia and apology as a response to a crisis?

Q99   How do I use PR to lessen the damage caused by a product recall?

Q100 How do I rebuild my organisation's reputation after a crisis?

Q97   Should the most senior manager always be the spokesperson during a crisis?

The face of your organisation during a crisis should be the most senior manager. The owner, CEO, managing director, or board chairperson can speak with the full authority of your organisation. This builds trust with publics and the media and ensures that a consistent message is relayed from your organisation.

Their roles also give them an overview of the organisation, from daily routines to complex operational procedures. Industry experience and connections give them the background to take control of the crisis.

Sometimes, departmental managers are selected as spokespersons, but their focus may be narrower and technical. Managers in engineering, scientific, medical or IT roles may slip into technical jargon at a press conference that the media do not understand. Though some journalists are specialised industry correspondents, most do not have a technical background and need spokespersons who can communicate clearly. No matter how committed the organisation is to communicating openly, a spokesperson who cannot be understood will give the impression that something is being hidden. Departmental managers' skills can be used behind the scenes, providing briefing notes for the main spokesperson, and communicating directly with regulators, corporate customers and suppliers.

All the organisation's senior managers should receive media training, as even the most capable of them in their day-to-day role may be poor at communicating with the media. Journalists are trained to tease out information in press conferences and interviews: being evasive, hostile or even too forthright are traits that need to be addressed. If, after media training, the most senior manager is still a risk, the organisation should consider an alternate spokesperson.

See also
Q92   What is a crisis?
Q93   What is crisis management?

Q94   How do I prepare to manage a crisis?

Q95   What goes in my crisis kit?

Q96   How should I respond to a crisis?

Q98   What is the difference between an apologia and apology as a response to a crisis?

Q99   How do I use PR to lessen the damage caused by a product recall?

Q100 How do I rebuild my organisation's reputation after a crisis?

Q98 What is the difference between an apologia and an apology as a response to a crisis?

An apologia is not an apology, although it might contain one. Put simply, an apologia is when your organisation responds to a crisis by defending itself. It is generally accepted that an organisation has a public persona, or an individual identity. The apologia, then, is a way of shifting blame from itself.

An apologia can work in a number of different ways:

- The organisation denies that it has caused the crisis and defends its operations – for example, an airline can blame weather conditions and air traffic controllers at an airport where one of its planes has crashed;
- The organisation accepts that it has caused the crisis, but limits the damage to its reputation by highlighting its good work in other areas – the airline can point to its fleet being more environmentally friendly than its rivals';
- The organisation can change the context of the crisis – the airline can blame the accident on trade union practices at the airport that affect passenger safety.

An apologia is risky. Unless your organisation is very certain of its facts and level of responsibility, it could be seen as aggressive and dismissive. This would result in a backlash with long-term repercussions for your organisation's reputation.

Saying sorry, especially when your organisation believes that it is being unfairly blamed, may be difficult. But a sincere, humble apology that accepts responsibility, promises restitution to affected publics, and changes in future behaviour is often what people want to hear.

In short, the difference between an apologia and an apology is the difference between 'sorry, but ...' and simply 'sorry'.

> **HINT**
> When writing a corporate apology, the right tone is crucial. Use natural language, even if it seems emotional: the apology should create a sense of empathy between your organisation and its publics.

See also

Q92   What is a crisis?

Q93   What is crisis management?

Q94   How do I prepare to manage a crisis?

Q95   What goes in my crisis kit?

Q96   How should I respond to a crisis?

Q97   Should the most senior manager always be the spokesperson during a crisis?

Q99   How do I use PR to lessen the damage caused by a product recall?

Q100   How do I rebuild my organisation's reputation after a crisis?

Q99   How do I use PR to lessen the damage caused by a product recall?

Product recalls happen for many reasons including contaminated food and medicines, mechanical defects and mislabelling. A recall poses a risk to your organisation's reputation. How it is handled can help restore confidence in your organisation, which should act voluntarily before being forced to by a regulator.

Immediately the problem arises, precise information should be reported to the regulator:

- What is the problem (tampering, defect, mislabelling, contamination, etc)?
- What is the risk to public safety?
- What product batches are affected, and where are they in the supply chain?
- Where was the product manufactured?
- Where were the ingredients or materials sourced?

Next, contact should be made with affected publics. An information campaign using direct contact, news media, social media, and advertising should begin. The campaign should:

- Be honest about the problem;
- Give exact information about the affected product;
- Avoid blaming suppliers or distributors;
- Apologise and say what is being done to prevent a recurrence;
- Acknowledge that the recall will inconvenience people;
- Give instructions for returning the product for a refund, repair or replacement – some form of compensation could be offered as a goodwill gesture;
- Publicise contact details for telephone or online customer support;
- Provide updates even after the recall has ended.

Employees should not be overlooked. Management should acknowledge their concerns about job losses, or their role in causing harm to somebody. Regular management briefings and counselling sessions, if needed, can address internal damage.

Johnson and Johnson's 1982 recall of its analgesic Tylenol, manufactured by McNeil Healthcare, is the touchstone for recall PR. Seven people died in Chicago after packs were poisoned with cyanide by an unknown person. The company withdrew all packs nationwide, incurring huge financial losses, but made a virtue of the recall by re-launching Tylenol in tamperproof packaging, reassuring consumers that it took their safety seriously. However, good reputations are not permanently won: in 2010, after 20 months of consumer complaints about side-effects, McNeil was forced to recall Tylenol while it addressed the problems.

See also

Q92   What is a crisis?
Q93   What is crisis management?
Q94   How do I prepare to manage a crisis?
Q95   What goes in my crisis kit?
Q96   How should I respond to a crisis?
Q97   Should the most senior manager always be the spokesperson during a crisis?
Q98   What is the difference between an apologia and apology as a response to a crisis?
Q100   How do I rebuild my organisation's reputation after a crisis?

Q100 How do I rebuild my organisation's reputation after a crisis?

The best way to have a good reputation after a crisis is to have a good one *before* a crisis. A positive reputation builds goodwill among publics, and this can offset the damage a crisis causes.

For an organisation that performed poorly in a crisis, restoring a reputation is hard. Your organisation must analyse its performance when the crisis is over. It should focus on how it is perceived by its publics, and how this perception can be improved. Change must be a real effort to address a problem, and not a sop to publics: changes in culture or safety standards, for example, must be followed through.

Poorly-handled media relations, either through disorganisation or giving wrong information, is damaging. Journalists' own reputations may have suffered if they were misled, even accidentally. Their attitude may be hostile, and reports on anniversaries, inquests or court cases may be more feared than welcome. Rebuilding reputation will require building efficient, truthful relationships. Taking the initiative and apologising to journalists individually may help.

Direct communication with publics also can help. Staff, shareholders, customers and suppliers, may respond positively to a letter from the CEO acknowledging that your organisation fell short, and outlining what it will do to improve in the future.

The organisation can position itself as a good corporate citizen by investing in corporate social responsibility (CSR) programmes, charitable sponsorships or community relations programmes. These are effective ways of showing that it is trying to make amends.

Your organisation may be damned no matter what it does. Genuine efforts to rebuild goodwill may be seen as cynical attempts to manipulate public sentiment. Yet, if your organisation does nothing, it will be criticised for being uncaring and unsympathetic. Reputations, clearly, are hard won and easily lost.

> **HINT** Sincerity is the crucial in rebuilding reputation. Sponsoring a charity should be done because it is the right thing to do, not because it is good to be seen doing it. Organisations that give unconditionally restore their reputations quicker.

See also

Q92   What is a crisis?

Q93   What is crisis management?

Q94   How do I prepare to manage a crisis?

Q95   What goes in my crisis kit?

Q96   How should I respond to a crisis?

Q97   Should the most senior manager always be the spokesperson during a crisis?

Q98   What is the difference between an apologia and apology as a response to a crisis?

Q99   How do I use PR to lessen the damage caused by a product recall?

ABOUT THE AUTHOR

Kevin Hora has taught public relations and political communication in further and higher education in a number of Dublin colleges since 2001. He holds a Postgraduate Diploma and Master's Degree in Public Relations from Dublin Institute of Technology, and a PhD in history from Trinity College, Dublin. His doctoral thesis was an examination of political public relations history in Ireland between 1922 and 1937. He also holds a Certificate in Training and Continuing Education from NUI Maynooth. A former *ex officio* member of the board of Dublin Chamber of Commerce, he is a member of both the Public Relations Institute of Ireland (PRII) and the European Public Relations Education and Research Association (EUPRERA). Married, he lives and lectures in Dublin.

ABOUT THE QUICK WIN SERIES

The **QUICK WIN** series of books, ebooks and apps is designed for the modern, busy reader, who wants to learn enough to complete the immediate task at hand, but needs to see the information in context.

Topics published to date include:

- QUICK WIN B2B SALES.
- QUICK WIN BUSINESS COMMUNICATIONS.
- QUICK WIN DIGITAL MARKETING.
- QUICK WIN ECONOMICS.
- QUICK WIN HR IRELAND.
- QUICK WIN LEADERSHIP.
- QUICK WIN MARKETING.
- QUICK WIN MEDIA LAW IRELAND.
- QUICK WIN PRESENTATIONS.
- QUICK WIN PUBLIC RELATIONS.
- QUICK WIN SAFETY MANAGEMENT.
- QUICK WIN SOCIAL MEDIA MARKETING.

See **www.oaktreepress.com** / **www.SuccessStore.com**

Lightning Source UK Ltd.
Milton Keynes UK
UKOW05f1619030214

225774UK00001B/3/P